The Impossible Road

From the First Seat In the Dumb Row to
My Own Private Island

Joe Massaro

I dedicate this book to my father and mother, along with my wife and two daughters for putting up with all the hours I wasn't home chasing the next big project.

Endorsement

"What Joe has accomplished in his lifetime would take most of us five lifetimes or more. The pattern for his success began as a child. He was always one to do things his own way, but ultimately, the job got done. He's the type of a guy that looks at a situation, realizes that something must be done to resolve the inherent problem, and then goes about the business of accomplishing his goals. Always looking to acquire the assistance and advice of those more knowledgeable, but also ready to forsake such advice to do what he thought was best regardless of the situation. His self confidence in his own ability as proven to be the intangible quality that separates Joe Massaro from most other men.

As a host, I find he could not be more hospitable. I've had the pleasure of staying at his home, A Frank Lloyd Wright masterpiece, his pride and joy. It is an amazing architectural accomplishment befitting a man like Joe who has accomplished such a great deal in his life. And boy, does he cook a mean breakfast!

It's never easy to be a self starter, a self motivator like Joe. I, an actor who has overcome numerous obstacles to reach this point in my career, can recognize that factor which separates him from others—unwavering confidence. Whether you're playing a game of chess with him or listening to his latest innovative ideas about architecture, it's all a learning experience. He simply does not like to loose. While building his house on Petra Island, Joe was told it was a formidable task at best, he proceeded. Ultimately completing his objective. This holds true for most of Joe's proceedings with others. I find him to be a brilliant man. One who is possessed with success in whatever field he chooses. He's out of the old school line of thought, "If you can't get someone to do it, do it yourself." He's been a source of inspiration and a friend.

Joe is a man for this time. The world would be a better place if we had more Joe Massaros!"

-John Amos
Actor

CONTENTS

CHAPTER I

The Early Years

My first memory of school was kindergarten. I had to make a mold of my hands for my mother, have a snack, and play with new friends. My teacher was nice and pretty, too, but it all went downhill from there.

Welcome to first grade at Catholic School… with Darth Vader —a nun who dressed in a black habit with a white hood—as my teacher. Suddenly, the fun was gone when Darth Vader wanted me to spell words and answer questions. She kept asking me even though she knew I didn't have the answer. Everybody around me kept raising their hand. *Why doesn't she just ask them the question?* I thought. *They* knew the answers! The second and third grades were the same. That's when I knew I was not made for school. I was hoping maybe 4th grade would be my salvation. Sister Mary Elizabeth was my teacher this time around. The first thing she said to me was, "Are you going to be as smart as your brother?" I already knew the answer to that question; she was going to figure it out real soon.

***

Meet my brother Donald. My older brother was born on the same day, June 27th, three years earlier than me. You would think

1

with the same mother and father (and being born on the same day), we would have a lot in common and be very similar... but not even close. We would never play together. He didn't want anything to do with me for years. It was as if we came from different planets. My brother would spend three hours studying the night before his test, while I could do it in 15 minutes. When my brother and I came home from school, my mother would ask my brother how he did on his test. My brother would tell my mother that the test was tough and there was no way he did well.

Then my mother would ask me, "Joseph, how did you do on the test?"

I'd reply, "Mom, no problem, it was a breeze."

When the test results came in, my brother's grade was a 96, and he would be depressed. My grade would be a 56. Since my test was a lot easier... I only needed to know half of the questions. My favorite test was the multiple-choice style. I knew at least half the answers; I could guess at the rest of them and have a good chance at getting 25 percent of them correctly, which would give me a passing grade of 75 percent. Too bad not all the tests were multiple-choice; maybe, then, I would've made a good weatherman since they only had to be right 50 percent of the time. If I could go to meteorology school, then I would be at the top of my class like my brother, and my mother would be able to brag about both of her children.

***

Meet my mother, Marie. She came from an Italian immigrant family of five children. She was a brilliant woman who also had "street smarts." She was quick to tell a joke and make people laugh. She was college material but never had the chance to go. Marie was the driving force of the family, and nothing got past her. We lived in the small town called Elmsford, about 40 miles north of New York City. When I was five years old, we moved into a new house just outside of town. It was a great neighborhood to grow up in. Our cousins lived right on our street, another cousin lived a few streets down, and there were plenty of kids within walking distance to play with. Our only requirement during the summers was that we had to be home by six o'clock to have dinner with the family. After dinner, we would rush outside playing until dark. I was only seven or eight when we would take our bikes and be gone for most of the day. My mother was a stay-at-home mom; she was home every day for me after school, which was great, but it meant that I couldn't get away with anything. If she suspected I did something wrong, she would say,

"Joseph… I know you're lying."

"I am not lying, Ma. I swear!"

"I know you're lying. Stick out your tongue, let me see."

If I showed her my tongue, she would say, "See! I told you, you were lying."

But if I didn't show her my tongue, she would still say, "See! I knew you were lying." It didn't matter if I showed her my tongue or not. Either way, I was lying! I could never win with her.

My mother would work with me on my schoolwork every night. She would try everything to motivate me to learn. It's not that I didn't want to learn; it was that I just couldn't. I felt terrible for my mother; she had one genius and one idiot (at least she had a good average). I felt so guilty that one night when she was going to help me with my spelling words, I wrote them all out on a piece of paper, cut them into tiny pieces, and stuck them to the bottom of the coffee table in the living room using my spit. That night, I told my mother I wanted to do my spelling words in the living room. I laid on the floor underneath the table. She was so surprised and happy that I could spell every word correctly. However, her joy didn't last long. The next day, when I brought my test back to her, of course, I had flunked it.

"Joseph, how did you fail that test? You spelled every single word correctly last night. That teacher must've made a mistake. I'm going to that school tomorrow to find out what happened. Is there anything you want to tell me before I meet with your teacher tomorrow?"

"What do you mean, Mom?" I said with guilt.

"What I mean is... I found all these little pieces of paper on the rug this morning when I vacuumed, you little son of a

4

bitch!" (That became my new name... 'son of a bitch.') That night, I was walking down the stairs, and I heard my mother say to my father,

"I don't know how Joseph is going to make it in this world."

"Don't worry about Joe, he will do just fine."

***

Meet my father, Carmen. Like my mother, he came from an Italian immigrant family of five, and his education ended at eighth-grade. When The Great Depression hit America, my grandfather sent my father, a teenager at the time, to a farming town called Red Hook, NY. Red Hook was about 80 miles north from where they lived, and my father was to run a gas station. My grandfather believed that the farmers were the only people with money during The Depression. My father learned how to repair cars, change oil and run the business. He once told me a story about his father visiting him up in Red Hook, and together they went to visit a farmer. After their visit, his father said to him,

"Carmen, why don't you date the nice farmer's daughter?"

"But Pop, she's got a mustache," my father replied.

"You don't have to kiss her, you just have to marry her!"

I always thought my dad got his sense of humor from his father. He was a quiet guy with a very dry sense of humor. Years later, my dad partnered with his brother in the garage in the town they lived in. My father did all the work while his brother got

5

involved in politics. Once my brother and I were born, my father let my mother handle the discipline in the family. On Monday nights, my mother would play cards with her girlfriends. It was our favorite time of the week. Before she left for cards, my mother would put us to bed. As soon as the door closed, my father would call us boys down to watch television, eat snacks and mess up my mother's living room with him.

One night, when we heard the door close, my father said the usual, "Come on down, boys." Little did we know that my mother was hiding around the corner waiting to bust our fun. She chased us upstairs with the wooden spoon. We couldn't believe our father did that to us, and boy did he laugh. I don't remember the whole story, but one day I did something that made my mom mad; it must have been bad because she would usually discipline us herself, but that time she said, "You little son-of-a-bitch, just wait until your father gets home." When my father got home, she gave him a hard time about not disciplining us and that he should do something about my behavior. He grabbed me by the hand, dragged me upstairs to the bathroom, and locked the door. He took off his belt and told me, "When I hit this tub, you start screaming." He and I went on for five minutes with him smacking the tub and me screaming. My mother ran up the stairs screaming and banging on the door, "You're killing him, you're killing him!"

When he opened the door, she looked at both of us laughing. He said, "Don't ever ask me to discipline this boy again." He did not like to yell at us, but I must say one thing... my brother and I both knew if our father told us to do something, we did it, no questions asked and never any backtalk. He never even raised his voice at me, but he didn't have to.

My father was a great mechanic and somehow landed a job in Saudi Arabia as a heavy equipment mechanic. He spent 18 months out of the country. At that time, if you spent eighteen months or more out of the country, you didn't have to pay US taxes on your income. While my father was away, my mother took care of both my brother and me, and she also got a part-time job. It wasn't common for women to work outside of the house back then, but my mother took every opportunity she could find to make her own money while my father was away.

When my father got back from his first 18 month tour, he asked my mother if there was any money left that he had sent her. He assumed that my mother had been using the money he earned to support us while he was gone. She handed him the bank book with every dime he sent home. She saved all of it for him. My father couldn't believe that my mother had earned her own money and saved everything he had sent her. My mother was no ordinary woman. After that first garage was established, he went back to

Saudi Arabia for another 18 months. My dad used all the money he earned in Saudi Arabia to build his second garage.

***

I was a pretty happy kid until report card days. Those were the worst days of my life. I couldn't hide my report card because my brother went to the same school, and he was glad to show my mother his report card. My mother would ask, "Joseph, did you get your report card today?" I would come up with excuses like, "I left it in school" or "It might be on the bus," but then finally I'd have to show it to her. You see, when you had passing grades, the teachers wrote them in black ink, but when you had failing grades, they made them obvious and wrote them in red ink. I have to admit my report card was a lot more colorful than my brother's; his was all black.

Spelling was my biggest problem. The first thing that goes if you can't spell is penmanship. I tried to cover up my lousy spelling by making my handwriting hard to read. Anybody who knows me will agree that to this day, my writing is still hard to read. Back in the 1800s, most Americans spelled like I do, phonetically. I don't know why they didn't leave it that way. All of a sudden, they put silent letters in words. Why? How did that help? Or what about words that are spelled exactly the same but sound entirely different, e.g., "I desert someone in the desert." What the hell is that? Also, why is newspaper one word and toilet paper two words? They can both be used for the same purpose. Thank God for spellcheck.

***

When I was ten, my parents told us they were having another baby. That was a big surprise... for all of us! To be honest, at 10 and 13 years old, having a new baby in the house didn't affect my brother or me very much. We continued with our own business for the next few years while my father spoiled my little sister rotten.

***

Meet my sister Maria. By the time Maria was three, she was such a pain that we had no choice but to be mean to her. Maria should write her own book about the things we did; she would probably make us look better than I could. Luckily, she outgrew all of her brattiness and became one of my very best friends.

Fifth grade was about the time when they figured out that I needed glasses. My mom took me to an eye doctor in White Plains, New York, about ten minutes from where we lived. My eyes were so bad that I couldn't even read the largest letter on the test. When I walked out of that office with my glasses on my face, I looked around the city. I said to my mother, "Mom, everything is so beautiful." I was amazed at how clear everything was. *Maybe my poor eyesight has something to do with my problem at school?* I thought. I'd like to believe that was the reason for my "colorful report cards," but as it turned out, my glasses had nothing to do with my bad grades. Instead of making me smarter, I ended up in summer school again and again! Although I was the guy that hated school, I had to attend not only in the winter but also in the summer; fifth grade, sixth grade, seventh grade, and eighth grade.

I remember my happiest days being in the winter when the radio told us the schools were closed because of a heavy snowfall. I would get my snow shovel and make some money. Also, I would cut grass in the summer and had a paper route. I used the money I earned to buy parts to build my go-cart, which I eventually used to deliver my newspapers. I was the fastest paperboy in town! My brother had a paper route as well; he lasted about a week and a half because my father got tired of driving him around to deliver the papers. Believe it or not, I was an altar boy serving mass and faking my way through Latin during church services. As an altar boy, every once in a while, I would participate in a wedding. Usually, we would get a nice tip from the wedding group.

One day after school, the other altar boy said to me, "You took the wedding that I was supposed to serve." I told him that the priest picked me and that I had no say in it. He didn't believe me, so he beat me up. It was the day I decided that I didn't like being beaten up, so I avoided conflict for the rest of my life. Instead of fighting, I learned to talk my way out of whatever I got myself into. Boy, did I talk a lot! If that didn't work, I ran. Lucky for me, I was a fast runner! As I got older, I made sure that my friends were big guys so that I could still mouth off and didn't have to run as often.

The fifth grade was the first time that I was interested in girls. I remember being invited to a house party one time. My mother took me to buy new clothes for the party; I bought powder blue pants, white buck shoes, and a yellow shirt. When I walked into the party, I heard some girls say, "Look at Joey." In summer school that year, I sat next to a pretty little blonde, and all summer, I didn't say a word to her. On the last day of school, I finally introduced myself. We went outside to have our mothers pick us up, and it turned out that our mothers knew each other. That was the beginning of our friendship.

By the time I got to the sixth grade, my hair was longer, and I dressed just a little bit better than I used to. I started to get some confidence in myself. That's when my sixth-grade teacher, Sister Mary "Mean" called my mother and told her that I wasn't paying attention in school and that I was getting a little too wild. "You should make him cut his hair," she told my mom. The next day my mother took me to the barbershop and made me get another buzz cut… there went my self-esteem.

The seventh and eighth grade were pretty much the same. My grades did not improve, and I had to go to summer school both years. Towards the end of the eighth grade, my parents wanted me to go to the same high school as my brother. It was a Catholic boy's school. I had no desire to go to that school. I wanted to go to the public high school where my friends were... and girls. You had to take an entrance exam to get into that high school, and I thought there was no way I could pass that entrance exam. The next thing I knew, I was accepted. My parents must have paid somebody off. With my grades, there was no way I could've gotten in.

When I started my freshman year at that all-boys school, my brother started his senior year. In senior year you could drive your car to school, and that's what he did. To say we were not close brothers would be an understatement. He wouldn't let me ride with him. Instead, I had to take two public buses to get there. Freshman year was no different from any other school year. My brother continued to bring his report card home with all A's, and I continued to bring home my very colorful report card. I failed my freshman year in that all-boys school, and I was back in summer school so that I could pass to the next year. Then, I failed my junior year in high school and went back to summer school again. When I went to reapply at that high school, they told me I did not have enough credits to stay. I could quit, or they would throw me out, so I quit. It was not the brightest time of my life, but it sure was fun.

When my friends and I were 15 or 16 years old, we would get somebody to buy us beer. About 15 to 20 of us would go underneath the thruway bridge and drink our beer. Somehow my mother got wind of this. On one night, in particular, she drove to that bridge yelling out the window, "Joseph, I know you're up there!" My cousin Joe Bo and I took off running to the other end of town. We were walking down Main Street when my mother pulled her car over and said,

"I know you were up there under that bridge with them other bums. I just don't know how you got here so fast."

"Ma I don't know what you're talking about."

I'm not sure she believed me, and I don't know why she didn't just make me stick out my tongue!

One hot summer night, me and the other 15 boys decided to go swimming. We went up to the school for the deaf because we knew that they had a pool. We stripped naked and went swimming in their pool. Some of the guys put a canoe in the pool and were making a lot of noise. Somebody said,

"Calm down, they are going to call the police."

"They can't hear us, this is the school for the deaf," someone else said.

Sure enough, ten minutes later, here comes a police car. We all scattered, running across the highway naked. The police officer was standing by the fence yelling, "I have your shoes, come back!" My friend Bob left his shoes there. The following night, we were swimming in another swimming pool on the other end of town. We walked home when a policeman we knew picked us up and gave us a ride back into town. In the backseat on the floor of the police car

were my friend's shoes! When we left the police car, we took them
with us. The police officer must have known we took them, but he
never said anything.

My sister Maria was, of course, the smartest girl in her class. I
started to think that maybe I was adopted, and they found me on
the doorstep. One day I asked my mother why they did not have a
photo album of me when I was a baby; they had one of Donald,
and of course, they had one of Maria, but none of me.

"What the hell are you talking about Joseph? I have baby
pictures of you," she said as she stormed away. She must have felt
bad because a few days later (that's how long it took her to find a
picture of me!) she showed me a new picture album with pictures
of me, Don and Maria. "See, I have baby pictures of you, Joseph."

My mother handed me the album. I must've been 11 years old
in the pictures she showed me.

"That's not a baby picture, Mom. I have teeth in the picture." I
broke her chops for the rest of her life on that one!

It turns out my sister was as smart as my brother. Once she
made it through her bratty years, she straightened up and became a
lawyer. Maria moved to Denver after college at NYU, and she
started her family there. I traveled to Denver a lot when I was
working with QuickPen, which allowed me to watch her three
children grow up. Every time I was in Denver after my business, I

would take them to Benihana's for dinner. They still remember that to this day.

CHAPTER II

My Teen Years

Some people would be sad to get kicked out of high school with two years to go but not me; I was thrilled. There were no more bus rides on public transportation, no more jackets and ties, no more nuns and priests. My new school had girls, and I had a new girlfriend. Yippeee!

***

Meet Barbara. It was the summer before my junior year of the new high school. That summer, I went to a few parties with some of the guys from my neighborhood and kept seeing the same girl... Barbara. I had noticed her around town before. She was pretty noticeable with her long hair and beautiful face, but she wasn't very talkative. By the end of the third party, I had won her over. We dated for some time, eventually married, and had two girls. It felt like I was starting a whole new life. I grew out my hair (finally), and I traded my thick glasses for prescription sunglasses; I wore them so often that people started calling me "Shade". I had a beautiful girlfriend.

On my first day of public school, I met with my guidance counselor to see what subjects I needed to graduate on time. He told me that I needed English and Math and to choose from the list of classes to fill the rest of my day with. For my morning classes, I chose auto body and fender at the Boces Trade School. I couldn't believe that I could take auto body classes in high school! My best friend from my neighborhood, Frank, signed up for auto body and fender too. For my afternoon classes, I took shop, driver's education, and my first drafting class.

My first car was a 59 Edsel. My auto body and fender class project was to do all the bodywork on my car and repaint it. That was the first time in my ten years of schooling that I received an A! My mother tried to motivate me in my early school years by saying that she would give me a 100 dollar bill if I ever received an A. I finally was able to make her pay up. I also received an A in my drafting class and my shop class. I can't say the same for English and Math, but I wasn't failing a class for the first time. After school each day, I worked for a washing machine repair company in town, rebuilding pumps, stocking shelves, and helping out. On Saturday and half a day on Sunday, I worked for my father in his garage pumping gas, doing tune-ups, breaks, and learning about the automobile industry. I found that working with my hands and solving problems was what I was good at. After 15 years of living in my brother's smart shadow, I was finally good at something.

My senior year of school was better than I had ever expected. I rebuilt and repainted Barbara's father's 55 Chevy convertible in my auto body and fender class. It came out so well that a friend of mine asked me to repaint his 55 Chevy too, which I did that year. Nobody had to wake me up to go to school anymore... I wanted to go! My teacher in the mechanical drafting class was my teacher in my shop class as well. He took a liking to me, and in my mechanical drafting class, he gave me a project for my senior year; I was to make a complete set of architectural drawings of the new middle school they just completed. It was an excellent project for me, and it introduced me to the world of architectural drafting and construction.

In the second year of my part-time job at the washing machine repair company, they sent me out into the field to do repairs in people's homes. That was a lesson on how to deal with people. I realized it was not a career that I'd be interested in for the rest of my life. I worked the night shift at my father's gas station between six and nine pm, but sometimes I would fill in at night if my dad needed me. One night, a guy came into the garage and asked if I could give him two dollars worth of gas. He didn't have any money on him.

"No, I can't do that," I said.

"My money is at home but I'll pay you back," he replied.

"I am sorry but I can't do that."

"Hey, I will leave you my spare tire then go home and get my money and bring it back."

I figured that was okay, so I gave him two dollars worth of gas, and I took the spare tire. My father stopped in later that evening to see how I was doing, and he saw the spare tire in the office. He said to me,

"What's that spare tire doing here?"

I told him the story, and he said, "That guy is never coming back. Look at the tire, there is not a piece of tread on it! Not only did you lose two dollars, but it's going to cost me five dollars to get rid of the tire!"

***

My friend Frank worked at the local grocery store as a checkout guy after school. When he would get off work at nine pm, we would meet at my father's gas station and work on our dragster race car. After we finished building it, we would race at the drag strip in Wingdale, New York, every Sunday. Every once in a while, we would test the dragster by racing up Main Street to my friend's house. We would hide the dragster in his garage on Sunday morning while the roads were empty. I believe that hobby kept us out of major trouble, and it was something we were both very interested in.

Our girlfriends were friends with each other, and they would meet us at the racetrack on Sunday afternoons. That same year, Frank and I got invited to go deer hunting in the Adirondack Mountains with a friend of ours who was a police officer in town.

It was about 250 miles north of our town, and we fell in love with the area. The following year, I talked my father into buying a piece of land up there. My father and I went partners with my friend Frank. We bought an old trailer and put it on the property. That was a place where we would go whenever we had free time over the next 50 years. It cost us five dollars to have a farmer move the trailer down the road about five miles and put it on our property. That was the best five dollars we ever spent.

It was getting closer to the end of my senior year of high school. I had a beautiful girlfriend, a trailer upstate, a sweet dragster, and some really great friends. Life was looking good, and my grades weren't too bad. One day after school, I told my mother I needed a book report for my English class to pass and graduate on time. She asked if I had read the book. I said, "No, here's the book. You can read it and write me a good report." It was "The Catcher In The Rye." A couple of days later, I told my mother she had to go to school. She said, "What did you do now, Joseph?" I said, "Nothing Mom, but my teacher wrote on my book report, 'Your mother did a nice job on this book report!' They need to fit us both for our caps and gowns because we are graduating." Years later, I read the book and truly enjoyed it. I think my mother was happier about me graduating high school than my brother making the Dean's list at Notre Dame and getting accepted into The University of California in Berkeley.

No more school, winter or summer. Yay! I was 18 years old, and I needed to decide what to do with the rest of my life. There were three partners at the washing machine repair company. They offered me a full-time job to go to work with them after high school. They liked how I worked, and my personality was great for their customers, but I turned them down. Then they offered me an equal partnership in their business. It was amazing that they offered me that position because I was only 18 years of age, but I still turned them down.

I stayed friends with them and continued working on all their vehicles, but I knew the washing machine repair business wasn't for me. I went to work for my father full-time, and I really mean 'full-time': 70 hours a week at a dollar an hour. I started my day at six o'clock in the morning and finished at six o'clock in the evening, six days a week. With my new full-time job, it was time to buy myself a car. My father had a friend at the Ford dealership. Although I was more of a Chevy guy, the new Ford Mustangs were just coming out, and that's what I ordered, a 64 and a half Mustang. My father cosigned the note, and I paid him every month for towards car payment. It was a three-year loan, and I think I paid it for four years; I am still not really sure about it.

I kept asking him, "Am I finished paying yet?" He would say, "A couple more payments." It must've been his way of getting even with me because I refused to pay rent while living in his house.

Whenever he asked me to pay him rent, I would say, "No, you made me, and you don't have to pay for my college. Now, who's your favorite?"

One day, when the gas station was slow, I put my car on the lift and started cutting off the exhaust system. My father walked into the shop and said, "What the hell are you doing? That's a brand-new car!" I said, "Don't worry Pop, the car just needs dual exhaust." He shook his head and walked away. About two weeks later, when he was not in the garage, and I had no work, I pulled my car in and started taking the engine apart. Of course, when I had the car apart, my father walked in again and said,

"What the hell are you doing now?"

I said, "I need solid lifters because it floats out at 8,000 revolutions per minute."

Again, he just shook his head and walked out. By the time I was done, my Mustang was fast. It was what they called "a sleeper"; nothing fancy on the outside, but I had the engine tuned and set up perfectly. My brother had a brand-new Riviera, and I kept bugging him to race me. He kept saying, "No way I am going to race that piece of junk." I kept bugging him, and finally, he agreed. He said, "Only once. When I beat you, don't ever ask me to race you again." We went to the place we used for our drag race, which was a straight local highway with very little traffic.

The drag race rules were simple: you went from a dead stop for a quarter-mile, and whoever got there first won. I let Don do the hand drop so he couldn't say I cheated. We pulled up side-by-side, came to a complete stop, and when he dropped his hand… we took off. The race wasn't even close; I blew his doors in. Afterwards, when we pulled into my father's gas station, Don jumped out of his car, yelling, "We have to go again. It's not fair from a dead stop, let's do it from a rolling start."

I said, "Don, you said only once, and you would never race me again. Your fancy Riviera lost against my piece of junk."

Don hated losing, especially to me, so he kept bugging me and begging me to race him again. I finally agreed to race him one more time. We went back to the same spot, except this time we went with the rolling start. We started to accelerate. When we reached 20 miles an hour, he dropped his hands, and we took off. I blew his doors in again, and I loved every minute of it.

My father used to call me 'Hose'. He claimed it was short for José. One day, he decided to buy personalized overalls with the garage logo on them for all of us to wear at work. The overalls finally came in, and the name written on mine said, in fact, 'Hose.'

I said to my father, "What the hell is Hose?"

He said, "That is short for José."

I said, "No, it's not, it says Hose!"

For a long time after that day, everybody called me Hose. My cousin Joe Bo still calls me Hose to this day! Like I said before, my father had an interesting sense of humor. Aside from his jokes, my father was a great mechanic. He knew his way around an engine was also a unique businessman. He charged more for gas at his gas station than any other station in town. If you complained about his gas price, he would tell you to get your car fixed someplace else. If somebody had a problem, they would come to see him. One day, a customer came into the station and said to my father, "Something's wrong with my car, it's running rough." My father opened the hood and listened to the car. He walked into the station, came back out with a tiny little hammer, and smacked the carburetor one time, and the problem went away.

The guy said, "That's amazing, Carmen. How much do I owe you?"

My father said, "Five dollars."

"Five dollars? For hitting the carburetor with a hammer?"

"No, I only charged you a dollar to hit the carburetor with a hammer, but I charged you four dollars to know *where* to hit it."

***

Life was being pretty good to me. I found my groove at my dad's station, working full-time as a pretty good mechanic. I could fix almost anything. I was working 70 hours a week, and on the weekends, I would drag race, go upstate to the camp, or drive around on a Sunday afternoon with Frank and our girlfriends.

My first race at a real track was against semi-pro dragsters. The race was entirely backwards. I was used to driving a car with four forward gears, but our new race car only had three gears. Being that was my first race against someone who wasn't just a friend but a real racer, I was a little nervous, and at the starting line, I accidentally put the car in reverse. When the light changed, and I popped the clutch, I was going backwards very fast. I stopped, shifted to the right forward gear, and I still won the race. In another race we had, we won our class; it gave us the chance to move up the ranks and race against the top class.

To my surprise, I was racing against the number one drag racer of that year, Don Garlits. He was the next up-and-coming racer, but now… look him up! He's considered the father of drag racing, known to his fans as Big Daddy, and I was racing him. In that race, we got a head start because of the difference in the classes. When the light changed, I took off. About three-quarters the way down the track, I still did not see my opponent. I knew I was going to win! I could already see that checkered flag in my mind. Then, I heard an awful noise and saw a flash go by me like a bullet…Big Daddy came out of nowhere and ripped that checkered flag right out of my hand.

***

Besides racing, Frank and I liked water skiing on Lake Mahopac in the summer. Mahopac was a town about 25 miles north of us that we discovered. It had a beautiful lake with three islands, and Frank had his boat at the local marina. We would ski all day in between two of the islands. The way we had a chance to ski was by driving the boat; if you knocked the other guy off his skis, you got the next turn. One of the islands we would ski around was a beautiful little heart-shaped island. We could not get close to that island because dogs would jump in the water and chase you if you got too close. After a full day of waterskiing, Frank and I would drive around the lake on the boat and look at all the rich people's houses, never imagining we could own something like them.

We decided we wanted to put an addition on the trailer upstate. We added a living room and a bedroom. We preordered all the materials and had them delivered to the campsite on the day we were planning to get up there. My father and his friend Slim came up to help Frank and me put on the addition. Slim was a laborer by trade. He could work all day long without ever getting tired. When we got to the camp, Slim said to my father,

"Carmen, how much land do you own up here?"

My father, standing in the road, swings his arm from left to right covering hundreds of acres, including two mountains, and says to slim, "I own all that."

27

We only owned a one hundred foot by one hundred foot piece of property. The following morning before we woke up, Slim had moved all the lumber from the road to the job site by himself. We started the construction that day. We set the foundation blocks, framed out the floor and the walls. My father's job was to point his finger and tell us what to do; he was good at that. We stopped working when it got dark. Frank and I slept in the new bedroom with no roof. I can still remember the sky and all of its vast glory. I sure did love that place. The next day, Frank and I went on the roof and installed the tongue and groove boards, then the tar paper, and finally all the shingles. All in one day. When we got off that roof, our knees were bleeding, but man, was it worth it. Now we had a real camp in the Adirondack Mountains.

On one of our trips upstate, Frank and I found a restaurant about 12 miles from the camp called Brooke Side. We were introduced to the restaurant owner by our friend Charlie Fisher, a policeman who owned the campsite next to us. The owner of the restaurant was Mickey Simbrick; he was a great guy. Frank and I were 17 years old when we met him, not quite drinking age yet. We went for dinner one night, and before he served us a drink, he would say, "Where are you guys going after this, to town or back to the camp?" As long as we were going back to the camp, he would serve us. One day, Mickey asked us if we were going fishing. We told him no because we didn't have a boat or any fishing gear with us. He said, "There's a boat in my backyard, take that tomorrow." We thanked him, but we didn't have anything to tow it with. He said, "It's already hooked up to my jeep. Take the boat and the jeep and have fun."

Frank and I spent the next 30 years going up to the camp on Thanksgiving week. It started out as a deer hunting week. Frank and I would leave the Friday before Thanksgiving since we would only miss three days of work in that holiday week. Our friend from school, Don Trier, would join us on the night before Thanksgiving. On his way up, Don would stop at my house and then Frank's house to pick up all the food we needed for Thanksgiving, pre-cooked by our moms.

Over the years, more people joined our Thanksgiving week of hunting. One year, a friend of Frank's cousin came to go hunting with us, his name was John Pulaski. That night, John went to town and came back to the camp at about 3:30 am. At 4:30 am, the alarm went off to go hunting, and John jumped up and went hunting. John became the fourth member of our Thanksgiving week crew. Anyone who could party like that was a shoe-in. One morning it was raining, so we decided to go to town instead of hunting. It was 8 am, and we stopped at a bar in town to start our day. The bar's name was Belvedere, and the bartender's name was Joe. He had polio as a child, and you could see its effects in the braces he used for walking. We all sat at the bar and ordered bloody Mary's. The bartender, Joe, said,

"No hunting today, boys? Is the weather too bad?"

"Yeah, we don't want to go out there and get wet," I said.

We spent most of the day at the bar. The following day at 8 am, we were back at Belvedere. Joe, the bartender, asked again, "How come you're not hunting today?"

"Well, it's snowing a little bit and the snow gets down the back of your neck. It's not a good day for hunting."

We spent another day at Belvedere, and the next morning, we were back again. The sun was shining, and Joe said to me,

"Why aren't you hunting today?"

I said, "Joe, with the sun shining and the scopes on the rifle, the sun could blind you."

From that time on, everybody in town called us 'The Hunters'. The drinking age was 18 years of age back then. There were about 17 bars in that little town near Paul Smith College. The four of us hunters drank Dewar's Scotch. Many local bars would order an extra case of Dewar's for Thanksgiving week because of 'The Hunters'.

***

I made many friends in the Adirondacks over the years. One night in Saranac Lake, I was separated from the group of hunters and wandered into a new bar named Friendly's Pub. I sat at the end of the bar, and the bartender—a big guy—came over and asked me what I wanted to drink. I told him I would take a Dewar's and club soda. He made my drink, set it down in front of me, and walked to the other side of the bar. Five minutes later, he came down to where I was sitting and asked, "Who the fuck are you?"

An hour later, we were sitting on the brass floor rail doing shots of Scotch. He was a local, and everybody in town knew him as 'Eggplant.' He had many nicknames, but his real name was Brad McDowell. We became good friends, and we influenced each other's lives in many ways throughout the years.

CHAPTER III

Starting My New Career

At this point in life, I was 19 years old and still working at my father's gas station. I had a lot of friends and a beautiful girlfriend. During my high school years, all I wanted to do was finish school and work in my father's gas station. After working there full-time for almost a year, I felt something was missing. There was no real challenge; most of it was routine work. Every once in a while, my uncle Vincent would come to get gas in his big fancy car. He would say to me, "Why don't you come work for me, Joseph? You can make a lot more money!"

Uncle Vincent owned a sheet metal shop and an air conditioning company that manufactured and installed ductwork for heating and air-conditioning. He said he could get me into the Sheet Metal Union, and I would only have to work until 3:30 pm every day. In my mind, there was no way I was going to leave my father, but his offer was tempting. After repairing Uncle Vincent's truck one day, I had to deliver it back to his shop. When I got there, he said to me,

"Come into the shop with me, Joseph, I want to show you something." He took me into the shop and said, "Look at these guys working here, they're making one of a kind sheet metal

33

fittings using raw materials. These sheet metal craftsmen are highly regarded and after a full day of work, they are all still clean. It is 3 o'clock in the afternoon and they're leaving in a half hour to go home. What time are you finishing tonight?"

"About 6 o'clock."

"Look at you, you're full of grease and you still have three hours to work… think about it."

To this day, I still don't know how I ever left my father! I kind of blocked it out of my mind because my dad and I had such a great relationship. I remember speaking to my brother about it, and he thought that our dad didn't want to see me in that same business; he knew how tough it was. My father and my brother were talking about the possibility of opening a Toyota dealership for me. Still, in order to do that, they had to purchase two automobiles upfront, and my father wasn't about to spend the money for that. Another mechanic was working at the garage with me, Eddie Foley. He was a good mechanic and a good friend, so it wasn't like I would leave my father without backup.

I finally decided to take the job at my uncle's shop. That first weekend there was a rush job at the General Motors plant in Tarrytown, NY, during their shutdown. It was all hands on deck. We worked 12 hours a day, seven days a week, and I spent my time inside a spray booth tank, cleaning the tank to get it ready for welding. I was never so dirty in my life. When I received my first paycheck that week, it was a dollar less than my father paid me with the taxes taken out. *So much for staying clean and getting off work early,* I thought. After that first week, I quit. My uncle persuaded me to stay around a little longer… that turned into 36 years!

***

Meet my new boss and uncle, Vincent Gervasi. He was my mother's brother, the youngest of five children and apparently the wildest. Sometimes in life, a simple misunderstanding can change the entire course of your life. My uncle once told a story of his mother that did just that. On this particular day, he and his mom were in a store when they ran into an old friend. This friend asked Vincent's mother how she was doing. Her reply was, "I would be doing great if it wasn't for this one." Although it was a common complaint for a mother with a rambunctious son, it haunted my uncle for the rest of his life.

He was a tough guy, maybe in part due to the weight he carried around thinking his mother would be better without him. It was almost impossible to change his mind about anything. He was a very smart man and a good businessman, but maybe a little lazy. When he was old enough, he joined the army before the war. After he was released from the army, he started hopping trains across the country. He took odd jobs and played poker to make ends meet. Vincent ended up in New Orleans looking for a job. One day he heard noises coming from a building, so he went to check it out. He was approached by the owner of what ended up being a sheet metal shop. My uncle asked the owner if he was hiring; he said, "Do you have any experience in sheet-metal?" and of course, my uncle said yes, even though he had none. A few workdays went by, and the owner said to him, "It's obvious you have no experience in sheet metal but you're a good worker so I'm going to teach you." That's how he ultimately got into the sheet metal business.

When he returned home to New York in 1946, he started his own business in the basement of his house. He named his company Elmsford Sheet Metal Works after the name of the town he lived in. I knew my uncle Vincent all of my life and as far back as I can remember. Every Sunday morning, he was at my house having fried meatballs with my mother and me before he went to play golf. He was a single man and had no children at that time. Every major holiday (Christmas, Easter, and Thanksgiving), the entire family would get together. Most of the holidays were celebrated at my parents' house.

As I got older, my cousin Joey and I would play outside, and Uncle Vincent would come by and ask, "Which one of you wants to come to the job site with me?" Most of the time, it was me because I was older than my cousin. I liked to go with him, not because I was interested in sheet metal installation, but because we needed nails to build our fort. I would stuff my pockets with nails when I was on the job sites. He was a good uncle. He took us to places like Playland, to baseball games, and things like that.

As Uncle Vincent's business grew, he moved from his basement in his house to a small building in the same town. A few years later, he sold that little building and moved into a larger one that he had built. Three days after he sold the building, a truck lost control and crashed into it, breaking the natural gas line. The truck driver got everybody out of the building just before it blew to pieces. There was nothing left but bricks. To say my uncle was a lucky man would be an understatement.

In his new building, he ran his first company, Elmsford Sheet Metal, and started a second company called Westchester Air Conditioning. Running two businesses kept him pretty busy. He built a bachelor pad for himself in the new office that my mother and their sister Carmella would clean for him once a week. Eventually, he got married to Mary Pellegrino. She was a sweet woman who sang opera. They had three daughters: Roseanne, Norma, and Martha.

***

Three months after I started working with my uncle Vincent, I was accepted into the apprenticeship program for the Sheet Metal Workers Union of Local 38. It was a four-year apprenticeship program that consisted of on-the-job training and a four-hour class every Monday night. The classwork consisted of laying out different types of sheet metal fittings. Now I know why I should've paid attention in geometry class. Suddenly, I needed to know that the hypotenuse was equal to the square of the sum of the two legs. Good thing I took geometry three times in high school.

Being a first-term apprentice working with mechanics that had been in the business for years, you better get used to harassment. As far as they were concerned, you had to do what they told you to do. You were not allowed to try to think because you didn't know diddly. The first job they sent me on was at Yonkers Raceway. We had to insulate the ductwork, which was about 25 feet up in the air. The foreman on the job had years of experience. His name was Pete Anules. The other mechanic's name was Dave Weber. When we got to the job site, the two mechanics started talking about how they would do the project. Pete said to Dave, "Let's throw a rope over the pipe up there, tie it around the kids waste (referring to me) and pull him up to the top." As mentioned, it was my first day on the job. I didn't know that they set up scaffolding to reach the high parts. They took a rope and threw it over the pipe, tied it to my waist, and started lifting me off the ground, all the while laughing in hysteria!

***

My next job was at the General Motors assembly plant in Tarrytown, New York, and Pete Anules was my foreman again.

The job was at least 30 feet up in the air. The second day on the job, Uncle Vincent showed up on the site and said to Pete,

"Where is my nephew?" Pete pointed upwards.

Vincent looked up and said, "If my sister would see him up there she would kill me."

"He has to learn sometimes."

***

The next job was at a brand-new junior high school in Port Chester, New York. For the first few months, it was just Pete and me. I enjoyed the work I was doing. Pete didn't go by the books; he let me make decisions and try things that other foreman would never allow. I was a good apprentice. On my hard hat, I wrote 'Super Apprentice' (that was way better than 'Hose'). One day, while I was working on a ladder, I had to adjust the duct by jamming it up with a support. The support slipped, and I cut my hand. Pete was working on the ground, so I yelled down and told him I had cut myself. Pete didn't even look up; he just told me not to worry about it and that we would take care of it after work. So I continued to work. Pete noticed that there was blood dripping all over the ground under where I was working, so he finally yelled up to me,

"What the hell did you do?"

"I told you I cut myself."

He yelled for me to get down so he could take a look at it. "You have to go to the hospital, you need stitches," he yelled.

He started giving me directions to the hospital then said, "Never mind… Get in my car, I'll take you there myself." I needed seven stitches in my hand. There was no heat, no windows, no tarps, just cold in the building. So cold that the skin cracked near the joints of my fingers. I couldn't wear gloves. I had to put Vaseline on my hands every night to heal them. As cold as I was, I loved what I did. One day we had to move some black iron ductwork (to be used for the kitchen exhaust) from where it was unloaded to where we needed it. Black iron ductwork was extremely heavy, so heavy that the drivers had sent an extra man to help unload it off the truck. They expected the two of us to install it by ourselves. After the delivery truck left, Pete told me to get some oil for his dolly because the wheels were not rolling well enough to move such a heavy load. He put the dolly upside down on a bench and waited for me to come back with the oil. I came back and said,

"Pete, I can't find any oil. Let's just move them."

He got mad at me and went looking for oil himself. I got mad at him, so I put the dolly on the ground, put the heavy piece on the dolly, and rolled it where it belonged. Then, I put the dolly back where Pete had left it, upside-down waiting for oil. Pete came back, oiled the wheels, tested them to make sure they moved easily, looked around, and said,

"Where's the duct?"

"It's in the room where it belongs."

He was not impressed. Instead, he told me to get off the job. I sat in my car for 20 minutes and then went back to work to listen to Pete give me hell. He didn't want me to do anything stupid like that because he knew I could get hurt. Firing me was his way of looking out for me. Towards the end of the job, more men came to the job site to complete the work. I was an apprentice for four mechanics.

The mechanics never had to ask for different tools or the next piece because I anticipated their needs and had everything ready. Every six months, I would get advanced to my next apprentice term as long as my schoolwork was done correctly. That was never a problem, can you believe it? I enjoyed what I was learning at this school, and I was good at it! With every advancement, I would also get an automatic pay raise.

***

In the second year of my apprenticeship, Pete and I had a brand-new high school to work on in Somers, New York, about 30 miles north of the shop. The first day on the job, I said to Pete,

"Let me have the drawings this time, Pete, let me start this job."

"Okay kid, it's all yours."

There were four offices. Three of them were typical, and one was a little different. The shop had prefabricated the sections of ductwork for each office. I ran around laying out the pieces. Pete and I spent the rest of the day installing the first one. When I went back to the office, I looked at the drawings and realized I put the pieces in the wrong office. I was a wise guy, so I said to Pete,

"Hey, Pete, you screwed up and put the pieces in the wrong rooms."

Pete didn't think I was funny, so he fired me for the second time. Pete and I spent the rest of the summer working on the job by ourselves; no roof on the building. There was sunshine all day long. I had a beautiful tan; it was a great summer. As more jobs opened up, more men came to work with us. The union rule was: if the job was more than x amount of miles from the shop, you would get travel expense money. I lived in the town where the shop was, so I would pick up three guys and use my car to take them to the job site in the morning. They would pay me two dollars each a day. That was a nice piece of change when I was making 1.25 dollars per hour. On Wednesdays after work, one of the mechanics, Ray Bassey, would go to the Bronx and pick up fresh Italian sausages for Thursday's lunch. I would start the barbecue in the morning when I got to work, and I would cook the sausages so they would be cooked perfectly by noon. On one Thursday, somebody said that our boss Vincent was on the job. I took the grill with the sausages cooking and went into a closet. When he came into the area where we were working, he said,

"What's that smell?"

"Oh it's the roofing tar," the guys said.

Then he asked, "Where is my nephew?"

"He's working in the basement."

It was so great working in the field because my boss was hardly ever there, and we were all working on our own. Sometimes, on the way back to the shop, in my car were Pete, Frankie Pal, and Harry Goldstein. On the way down the Saw Mill River parkway, Harry once said to me, "Let me see how fast this car is." We were in my souped-up Mustang. I put the gas pedal to the floor, bringing us to 100 miles per hour in under a minute. Frankie Pal was on the floor screaming at me, and Pete threatened to turn off the ignition. Every few days, I would do it again. Pete liked me. I was working on a job with Pete early on when he noticed I had holes in my shoes. He took me to a store and bought me a new pair of work shoes. He was a really nice guy.

Towards the end of this job, Uncle Vincent came to the job site and told Pete,

"I'm taking Joe away from you."

"You finally gave me a good kid and now you're taking him away, I quit!" Pete said.

"I'm not taking him away from you, Pete. I am giving him to some other foremen; I have plans for this kid. I want to teach him the other parts of the business."

Pete didn't quit. I knew nothing of my uncle's plan for me. All I knew was that I enjoyed what I was doing, and I thought my career would lead me to be a foreman out on the field. That was my goal.

CHAPTER IV

My New Career

It was the year 1965, and I just had gotten moved from field-work to shop-work. Barbara, my girlfriend of five years, and I were planning a wedding. Well... she was planning a wedding, and I was going to show up!

Working in the shop and working in the field were two completely different jobs. Working in the field entails moving from job-site to job-site; you have to work with different types of buildings, different locations, and various types of trades. The standard hours in construction were between 8 am to 3:30 pm. In the field, I'd get a 15-minute coffee break in the morning which usually lasted 25 minutes, a 30-minute lunch break which generally lasted 45 minutes, and a 15-minute break in the afternoon. I was supposed to start work at 8 am, but it was usually 20 after eight before I'd get going. Quitting time was at 3:30, but I'd start cleaning up at about ten after 3.

Working conditions could be a challenge. The buildings had no heat and were not closed in when we were installing our work. Most of the work was on scaffolding or ladders. In the field, you could be unloading the truck in the rain, moving the materials to the part of the building that it goes into, installing ductwork up high, setting up equipment, and various other things.

Working in the shop was much different. Work started at 8 o'clock. I'd get a 15-minute coffee break in the morning, 30 minutes for lunch, and I stopped working at 3:30. I would work in a safer environment, warm in the winter and not too bad in the summer. I would work on smaller parts of the duct system and usually do the same job every day. You could be a layout man, the mechanic who develops patterns for the fitting. You could also be a brake man, the mechanic who bends the pattern into a shape. You could run the machines used to assemble the duct or become a fabricator who puts the ductwork together.

***

I started the third year of my apprenticeship working in the shop. My job was to lend a hand to whoever needed it; I could be loading the truck, making small connector pieces, learning to run all the different machines, or working on the dumb end of the power brakes. The power break was probably the most dangerous piece of equipment in the shop. The machine was used to bend metal. The job at the dumb end of the power break was where I would line up the dots on the metal to the center of the die and hold that spot while the operator would step on the pedal. Then, the break would come down and bend the metal. The only other important part of the job to remember was to keep your fingers out of there! I was working the dumb end of the power break with the shop foreman.

***

Meet Slim Johnson. Slim was the shop foreman for Elmsford Sheet Metal. His job was to oversee the workers and assign them the project he wanted to be done. He also interacted with the field on what they needed on their job site and set up workflows to get the suitable materials to the right job. He was also a layout man. His father, Frank, worked as a layout man with us too. He was almost 80 years old and was quite a gentleman, but Slim could sometimes be tough. If you messed up, he would make sure you knew it. He was also good at harassing you, but I was used to that after two years in the field. One day I worked with Slim on the dumb end of the power break; we were working on bending a bar slip that is used to connect two pieces of duct together. It took about five bends and three die changes to make it, but it was very time consuming. After about an hour on the dumb side of the power break, I said to Slim,

"Slim, I think we can save one die change."

"Kid, I have been doing this job for 20 years. You are nothing but a third term apprentice. Just do your job on the dumb side of this break." So, I went back to my work, keeping my mouth shut. Another 30 minutes went by, and Slim said to me,

"Okay, smart ass, show me how you would save one die change."

"If we bend one and three first, then we only have to change the die once," I said to him.

He looked at that very carefully and said,

"Son of a bitch, you're right!"

I was always pretty good at seeing where I could cut corners and save time! Eventually, I learned to run all the equipment in the shop. I learned to weld, fabricate, and finally layout the pattern for the fittings. I still missed working in the field, but I settled into my new job as a layout man.

I was just about finished with the third year of my apprenticeship when my uncle came out to the shop and asked, "Does anybody have any drafting experience?"

"I have some experience!" I said.

In my senior year of high school, I completed a set of architectural drawings in my mechanical drafting class, remember? Not quite the same, but enough to get me started. So my uncle moved me again to another part of the business.

At the time, we were doing some smaller commercial jobs and installing air conditioning with Vincent's other company, Westchester Air. Typically, an install job would need four or five different people working their specialty to complete the job. But on some of the smaller house projects, I would go to the home to measure existing conditions, make the set of drawings, fabricate all the ductwork, and install the job. Technically, I was working four different positions by myself, and I was doing it fast! One day, my uncle asked me if we had a problem on the job.

"Why are you back here so early?"

"We finished the job," I said.

"No way... you went there this morning!"

"Do you want me to go back to the job and wait until 3:30?"

He shook his head and walked away. I worked like that for the following four jobs, learning each position and getting a little better each time.

***

I started my fourth and last year of my apprenticeship in 1969. Barbara and I were married for two years and had been living in an apartment in Valhalla. We had been saving money to buy our own house and even saving change in a piggy bank! Every weekend, we would look at homes for sale and take my father with us. Every home we liked, he didn't like. It was getting pretty frustrating. We didn't pay much attention to what was wrong with these houses because we just wanted to buy one. We became so frustrated with all the problems my dad kept finding with the homes that we decided to stop looking and just stick with our apartment for a while longer. Eight months later, my father called me up and said that two guys he knew built a house in Lincolndale and were trying to sell it. Lincolndale was about 35 miles from Elmsford. It was a brand-new high ranch on one and a half-acre of land. We fell in love with it and bought it on the spot. To this day, I'm so glad we listened to my father about the other houses; it turned out that he knew what he was talking about.

We used all the money we had saved for our house's down payment, even the quarters my wife had saved from her tips as a hairdresser. We ate dinner at my parents' house for the next three months because we were too broke to buy food, but it was worth it. We had the house we wanted. With the new house, we had almost an hour drive to work. I started work at six am in the morning but my wife, a hairdresser in Elmsford, didn't start until nine am. Since we only had one car, she would get up at five in the morning with me and we would drive to Elmsford together. I would drop her off at her girlfriend Terry's house where she would get dressed and go to work from there. I would finish work at three thirty and she would work until seven, Tuesday through Saturday. I would hang around my parents' house until she got off work, and we would drive home together.

***

In 1968 the Vietnam War was just ramping up. I had heard nothing from the draft board until that August when I received the classification of 1A, which meant that I was prime material for the draft. We had sent a letter to the draft board looking for a deferment since we did government work at West Point. We did not hear anything from the draft board. Finally, I received a draft notice from the Army in March of 1969. I was 23 years old, and I was directed to report to Whitehall Street in New York City in two weeks to prepare for immediate induction into the US Army.

There was no way my wife could make the mortgage payments on the new house with her salary alone. We had friends that lived in an apartment, and they agreed to move into our house. Their rent would've helped us keep afloat until I was back to work. My job gave me a big going away party. I only saw my father cry twice in his life; the first time was when his father passed away, and the second time was when I got drafted. He said to me, "I might be able to fix this!" One of his brothers was a politician and very friendly with Governor Rockefeller. I told him, "No, I'll do my duty."

The morning that I reported to White Hall Street, three other boys from my town were there too. The four of us went through the different departments at Whitehall. They dismissed the other three boys at the end of the day because all three had felony records. Late that afternoon, I was sworn in and put on the train to Fort Jackson, South Carolina. The train was packed with 18-years-old new draftees. I was 23 years old at the time. It was the longest train ride of my life! I was very apprehensive and didn't know what to expect. I knew one thing though… that there was no doubt I was going to Vietnam. It was probably the only time I felt all alone in the world. The only one who knew I was scared was myself. It suddenly felt like I no longer had control of my life.

**

March 1969.

Welcome to Fort Jackson, South Carolina, the reception center for the United States Army. My first day in the army was a whole lot of hurry up and wait. The second day, while I was standing in line for a haircut, I heard my name being called out. I couldn't imagine why they were calling my name. I didn't think anyone knew who I was. I acknowledged that I was Joe Massaro, and a soldier who I didn't know said, "Come with me." I followed him into an office. They put me in a little room by myself without telling me what was going on. *This kind of silence means that there has been a tragedy at home*, I thought. A few hours later, the door opened, and I was told to go into the office. There was a captain sitting behind a desk who said to me,

"Who's your father, Senator Fulbright? I got more calls about you then anybody on this base."

"Sir, I have no idea what you're talking about. All I know is I was told to report here," I replied.

The captain said there was a mess up on my paperwork; I wasn't supposed to be drafted. He continued explaining there was a general from New York on the phone, and he wanted to talk to me. I picked up the phone, and the general said to me,

"The day you left home there was a postponement of induction in your mailbox."

"General, if this is just a paperwork mess up and I'm going to have to come back here, I might as well stay," I said.

The captain behind the desk kept shaking his head and said,

"Yes, you're coming back here."

The general said to me, "I can't tell you what to do, boy, all I can tell you is what I would do."

"What would you do, General?"

"I would get my ass out of there as fast as I could."

I thanked the general and hung up. Right then and there, I said to myself that if the general was giving me this advice, I better listen to him and get my ass out of there as fast as I could. The captain then said to me,

"What are you going to do?"

"I'm leaving, sir."

"You can leave now on your own, or you could wait until this afternoon and we will drive you to the airport."

"I'm leaving now!" I said and started walking out of the gate with my orders to report back to Whitehall Street the next day.

I walked through the gate past a female soldier when she said, "Where are you going, soldier?"

"I'm going home!"

That was my first ride on a jet plane, and I loved it. I found out later that the general was a friend of my uncle, who was a friend of Governor Rockefeller. My dad got me out of there, after all.

I got home late that night and had to report back to Whitehall Street the following day at nine am, which was a Saturday. When I got down there, the doors were locked. I sat on the steps and waited. A little while later, an army officer came by and asked,

"What are you doing here?"

I said, "I have orders to report here today."

"Whitehall is not open on Saturdays, come back on Monday."

I returned Monday morning to start the process again, but nobody knew what to do with me; they kept sending me to different offices. It must've been at least five of them. In the last office, the captain looked up my paperwork and said, "I don't know what to do with you. You took the oath, so technically you're in the army. They messed up your paperwork so then you're not in the army." He told me to go home. And that's what I did. I realized what the term 'fubr' means in the army; 'f….. up beyond repair.' That was my situation, and nobody in the office knew how to fix it.

The next day, I went back to work and explained to everybody why I was here and not in the army. It was a little embarrassing after they gave me that nice party. Several weeks after getting back, I received a second draft notice telling me to report to Whitehall Street in two weeks for immediate induction into the army. Here we go again. I did not complain about it because I knew this was going to happen. Someone at work told me they read in the newspaper that the National Guard was looking for recruits. That was very unusual; everybody was trying to get into the National Guard, so they didn't have to go to Vietnam. I went right down, took the test, and was accepted to the New York National Guard.

The problem was if you already had a draft notice, they couldn't take you. I told them about my draft notice and asked if I could get it changed, would they take me then. They accepted, and I went to my draft board office to talk with them. I didn't think I had much of a chance, but I was going to try. I met with the Supervisor of my draft board; she was an older woman, and when I told her my name, she was not happy to see me. She said,

"You knew you were getting a postponement of induction and you went anyway."

"I did not know. I was on a train going to South Carolina. I had no idea. My wife received the notice in the mail after I left."

"I have more grief over that than any other thing I've ever done in this office."

"I was accepted into the National Guard and they will take me if you release me from this draft notice."

"Are you willing to spend six years in the National Guard?"

"Absolutely."

"You are such a pain in my ass that I will release you just to get you out of my hair."

It worked! I was out of the army and in the New York National Guard. Sometimes, being a pain in the ass pays off. I might not have been the sharpest tool in the shed, but I sure was the luckiest.

***

In 1970, the company was doing so well that my uncle decided to move to a larger building 30 miles north to Peekskill, New York. The location was much closer to my new house. My wife took a job in the town we had moved to. Our commute to work was a lot easier now. Since I would be leaving my job in a couple of weeks for basic training, I couldn't take on any large drafting jobs. Instead, I created layouts for the offices and the drafting department in ESM's (Elmsford Sheet Metal) new building. I also did the layout for all the shop machinery in the new space. I completed all of this work before I left for the army. Two weeks before I left, I decided to start exercising, so they didn't beat me up too badly in basic training. After work each night, I would drop the car off where my wife was working—about two miles from my house—and I'd run home to get myself in shape for what I knew were going to be a tough few months.

CHAPTER V

G.I. Joe

At the beginning of January 1970, I took the oath to join the Army National Guard. It was the second time I took that oath, but this time I was staying. I was assigned to a radio relay outfit in Orangeburg, New York, about an hour from my house. I was thrilled to be in the National Guard; the chances of getting activated and sent to Vietnam were minimal. I had to spend one weekend a month in training and two weeks in the summer at different army posts for six years.

On March 17, 1970, the New York Post Office went on strike. Remember that minimal chance of us getting activated? You guessed it. We were activated only two months after induction to deliver the mail. I hadn't started training yet, and I hadn't even been assigned a uniform yet! For the next two weeks, I had to stay at the armory while the other guards delivered the mail. The strike ended within two weeks, and they deactivated our unit. Within a week from that time, I was scheduled to start my basic training and spent the next six months away from work and home. It certainly was much better than spending a year in Vietnam.

***

April 1970. I was back at Fort Jackson, South Carolina, the reception center for the United States Army. Why does that sound familiar? This was the same place where I was two months prior, standing in line for a haircut. This time they cut my hair. The first three days in the reception center were pretty easy. We slept in air-conditioned brick barracks. For breakfast, you could have your eggs over easy or how you wanted. Most of the day was filled up by testing and paperwork. We received a duffel bag full of our equipment. During this time, I met another New York National Guard recruit that was in the same outfit as me but at a different armory in New York.

***

Meet Ronald Morrison from Yonkers, New York. We instantly became friends and were assigned to the same barracks in basic training. We are still friends 50 years later.

Day four: We were all sitting on our duffel bags, waiting for the trucks to take us to Tank Hill, the Army's basic training area. Even though we were national guards, we trained with the regular Army. Eighty-five percent of our basic training group would end up in Vietnam. There must've been hundreds of us sitting in the field smoking and joking when all of the sudden we heard a rumbling: 2 1/2 ton trucks stopped in front of us. There was complete silence; you could hear a pin drop. Five minutes later, they opened the back flap of the trucks, and drill sergeants jumped out of the back of the trucks and started screaming at everybody.

The drill sergeants walked up and down the rows of new recruits, kicking some of the fat guys off of their duffel bags while screaming, "Your easy days are over now, boys." It was pure chaos. They were yelling, "Pick up your duffel bags... put them down! You're too slow! Pick them up! Put them down!" Over and over for 30 minutes. They loaded us in the trucks and closed the back flap. Not a sound was heard. They drove us around for an hour, later to find out that the destination was only 10 minutes away!

The trucks came to a stop. Nobody moved or made a sound. The flap on the back of the truck was thrown open and an army sergeant wearing a hat like 'Smokey The Bear' started screaming, "Get out of the truck! Get the fuck out of the truck! Get in line!" One hundred new trainees were suddenly running around in circles while sergeants were screaming. Nobody knew where to go or what to do! This lasted for an hour. We finally got to our barracks and were assigned our beds and lockers. We were told to set up our lockers while 'Smokey The Bear' screamed at us, ripping stuff out of the lockers and telling us we were doing it all wrong, without ever telling us how to do it right.

Most of the guys were only 18 years old, and they had never experienced anything like this in their young lives. On the other hand, I was 24 and was at least used to all the hell I was put through by the old foreman on my jobs; not exactly the same, but I was no pushover. Next, they had us make up our cots. When you thought you were done and it looked good, they would find something wrong with it and rip it apart to make you do it again, over and over and over. When they really wanted your attention, they would get about an inch away from your face and scream at you.

Outside, there was a line drawn on the pavement in front of our barracks. Whenever they told us to 'fallout', we were supposed to line up on that line and stand at attention. When we were told to fallout, everybody would run to the door and try to line up as fast as they could. Nobody knew where they were supposed to stand. So for the next hour, we would practice 'falling out', which meant running to the line, lining up, and coming to attention, over and over again while being screamed at.

Finally, it was lunchtime. We were told whenever we were outside our barracks, wherever we were, whatever we were doing, we must run... not walk. So, we were now running to the mess hall, and when we would get there, we would stand in line. We were allowed to enter the mess hall four at a time and were instructed not to talk. All we did was take our trays, get our food; you had five minutes to eat and then get out. I was a fast eater. I had no trouble eating in five minutes, but most of the other troops could only get halfway through their food. We spent the rest of the first afternoon learning how to stand at attention. Dinner was the same routine. Just five minutes to eat dinner.

After dinner, we would meet our drill sergeant in the barracks: 24 recruits per floor and two floors per barracks. The drill sergeant picked the biggest recruit to be in charge of the rest of us. That night, we had to get the barracks ready for inspection for the next day. Our new temporary sergeant told us what we needed to clean. Lights out at ten o'clock, and I was ready for sleep. We found out that we needed a fire watch every night on each floor. That meant two men on each floor had to watch for fire for one hour every night. The first night, I ended up with fire watch between 1 am, and 2 am. You had to get up and get completely dressed before your fire watch.

The next morning they woke us at 4:30 am to start our day. We got dressed, ran to the parade field, and cleaned up old cigarette butts for an hour. Then it was off to our five-minute breakfast, then two hours of exercise. The rest of the day was marching and taking required medical shots. Later that morning, we found out that we came in last in the barracks inspection. Our drill sergeant was not a happy camper, and he let us know about it by screaming at the temporary sergeant. It turned into extra work because we failed inspection, and this pretty much summed up the routine for the first week. The worst part for me was that I was getting sick from their medical shots and could have used a night of sleep instead of waking up almost every night for an hour of fire watch. I needed to develop a plan, and there were several ways that basic training could be approached.

One way was to try to fight the system. During that first week, one of the recruits tried that. One day the drill sergeant told the recruit he wanted him to dig a hole five foot by five foot by four foot deep underneath the barracks. He was under there several hours. When he finally came out, the drill sergeant handed him a pack of matches and said, "Bury them." The recruit went back under the barracks and spent the next hour burying the matches. When he crawled out from under the barracks hot and dirty, the drill sergeant was standing there with a cigarette in his mouth; he said to the recruit, "Where's my matches?"

Another way to deal with basic training was to become a ghost. For the first week, my drill sergeant didn't even know my name. The only problem with this was that I was still on fire guard duty at night and not getting enough sleep. The temporary sergeant that my drill sergeant appointed to be in charge of us did not have to wake up for fire guard duty. Also, instead of sleeping with 24 other guys, he had his own room in the barracks. That was the way I wanted to deal with basic training... I needed his job! One day, I happened to be in the barracks when the inspector came in to give us our inspection. Our temporary sergeant had us polishing the

floors half the night, so we were hoping we would pass this time.
We came in last place again. After watching the inspection process,
I knew why we were failing, and I knew how we could correct it.
At the beginning of the following week, we were training
somewhere, and the sergeant gave us a break. My drill sergeant
was getting a drink of water. I went up to get a drink next to him
and keep in mind that I was still a ghost; he didn't even know my
name yet. I looked over at him, and I said,

"Excuse me, Sergeant, I can't help but notice that we came in
last every day last week for inspection."

He turned, looked at me, and said, "Yeah I know, what about
it?"

"If you put them stripes on my arm I'll get you in first place
every day."

I was no longer a ghost. I was taking a big chance here. If I
didn't get us in first place, it could've turned out very bad for me. *If
he thinks I'm just another New York wise guy, basic training could
be much harder for me*, I thought. He looked at me hard, called
over the temporary sergeant, ripped the stripes off his arm and
slammed them onto my chest, and said to me,

"You're my bitch now."

"I need one thing," I said.

"What's that?"

"I need to pick my second in-command."

"Alright!"

So I picked my friend Ronnie Morrison. I thought I might have a problem with the temporary sergeant I replaced. To my surprise, he was a happy guy because the drill sergeant and the other trainees stopped screaming at him. I knew I had to perform, or I was dead meat for the rest of basic training.

***

Meet Sergeant Ackens, five foot and ten inches tall, built like a tank. Probably 30 years old and two tours of duty in Vietnam. He was married and lived off base. I was sure I saw him on some recruiting poster. That night, I met with Ronnie, and we came up with a plan to clean the barracks. We assembled the rest of the men in our barracks. I introduced myself and Ronnie, then told them what we expected from them and how we were going to come in first place in every inspection. Ronnie and I set up work details giving each group a task we wanted them to complete. We had the barracks ready for inspection in half the time it usually took us. That was the first good night sleep I had all week. *No more fireguard for me, I hope!*

The following day we were up at 4:30 am. At five o'clock, we were back in the parade field picking up old cigarette butts. We'd been picking up cigarette butts for weeks now. Nobody could smoke that much overnight! I believe that while we were sleeping, they would go throw the cigarette butts back on the parade field so that we could pick them up again. At six o'clock, we were back in formation, getting ready to go to breakfast. While we were at breakfast, they inspected the barracks. After breakfast, we were back in formation and waiting for the inspection results; it was a make or break moment for me. They announced that our barracks came in first place for inspections that morning. I could see a slight smile on my drill sergeant's face, and I heard a sigh of relief from the men behind me.

That morning, we had to do a two-mile run; they timed us to see what kind of shape we were in. Before I went into basic training, I ran home after work every day, so I thought I was in pretty good shape. With about half a mile to go, I got a pain in my side, and I thought I was going to die. I could see the drill sergeant watching me, so I struggled through the finish. A lot of guys couldn't finish that run. Ninety-five percent of these trainees didn't want to be there. They were drafted and had no choice. The rest of the day was calisthenics, marching, and drilling. Depending on the day, it could be rifle training, hand grenades, bayonet practice, or more marching and drilling. As the weeks went by, the training became more and more intense. One night they marched us to this big field filled with sand, barbed wire, and explosives. The training was to climb the rope ladder over the wall, crawl under barbed wire, make it to the other side about 100 yards away while 50 caliber machine guns fired live ammunition over our heads.

The machine guns were fixed in a straight line high enough not to hit you unless you stood up. All was quiet when the sergeant yelled, "First wave on the wall." The first wave was about twenty guys all going over the wall first. The second wave on the wall was called to go as the first wave started under the barbed wire, which was when the gunfire started. Bullets were flying over our heads. Every once in a while, there would be an explosion next to us. I was in the third wave waiting to go over that wall, and Ronnie was right next to me. As I crawled over the wall, I bumped into the first two waves, which were jammed up right in front of me, under the barbed wire. There were only a couple of spots in the barbed wire that you could get under, and everybody was trying to go through the same spot. The machine gun fire was left and right, and nobody was willing to crawl under them. Every fifth bullet was a tracer, so you can see these bullets coming at you.

"Let's go under that gun, we will get out of here quicker," I said to Ronnie.

He didn't say anything and just followed me by crawling underneath that gun. You could feel the bullets going over your head as we were under the guns. We had the rest of the field open to us. We were the third wave over that wall and the first two guys sitting on the bleachers at the other end of that field drinking water. We were there for half an hour before anybody else got there, and our drill sergeant was aware of that.

A few days later, they sent us out into the woods with BB guns. We were on patrol looking for the enemy; snipers were hiding all over the place with BB guns. My drill sergeant made me one of the snipers. I camouflaged myself, and as the patrol came by, I shot the first guy, and the rest would scatter; it was kind of fun. My drill sergeant came by my position the second time. He said to me,

"You shot me in my ass when I went by!"

I said, "No, I didn't, Drill Sergeant, but I'm going to shoot you now."

I shot him with my BB gun. He took his BB gun, walked straight to me, and fired as many shots as he could. Thank God I had a face mask on. I had more lumps on my fingers than I could count. Whenever there was a new weapon to be trained on, my drill sergeant would let me demonstrate the weapon first. The twin 50 caliber machine gun was amazing. Not everybody got to fire the different weapons, but I got to fire them all.

The next training was with gas masks. They showed us how to put them on and fit them to our faces. Then, they drilled us for half a day on putting them on, clearing the mask of any gas, and taking them off. At the end of the training, we had to put a gas mask on and go into a building that was full of gas. To prove to us that the gas masks were working, before we could leave the building, we had to take the mask off and tell them our name, rank, and serial number. Do not believe what you see in the movies where they hold a handkerchief over their nose when the room is full of gas. What a shock it is when you are forced to take a breath of that gas before getting out of that room. It was like nothing I had ever imagined. It was so bad that many of the guys were throwing up when they go out.

When we were going on our night maneuvers, somebody told us that we would get hit with teargas. We were patrolling on a road in complete darkness; we had our gas mask with us, and sure enough, in came the teargas. I took my mask out and put it on in record time. The one thing I forgot to do was to clear the gas out of my mask before breathing as we were trained to do. What a shock that was! Panic everywhere. Everybody was running in different directions because they couldn't get the masks on and did not want to breathe in the gas. During that episode, I banged into somebody. I couldn't see who it was; it was pitch black. When it was over, and we were back in the light, I saw my drill sergeant; his eyes streaming with tears, yelling,

"Who was the son of a bitch who knocked the gas mask out of my hands when I tried to put my mask on?"

I waited until the last day of basic training to tell him it was me.

Towards the end of our basic training, they took us on a ten-mile hike with full packs and our rifles in the June heat. We were sweating like pigs. Every once in a while, I would see my drill sergeant walking alongside us, his uniform perfect, no sweat stains, and no wrinkles. It looked like it just came out of the dry cleaner. I found out later that he would drop back behind us and disappear. Then, he would show up a half-hour later after he went back to the barracks and got a ride back to where we were. To graduate from basic training, every man had to run two miles in a certain amount of time. By this time, I was in the best shape of my life. I had lost 15 pounds during my basic training. I was only135 pounds when I started, and I was now basically muscle and skin. I started the two-mile run with my drill sergeant timing me. As I ran by my drill sergeant, he said to me,

"You're not going to make it, Massaro, you are going to be recycled."

Recycled meant that you were going to have to do basic training over again. I looked at the drill sergeant, turned around, and ran backwards for a little while. I had no problem completing the run, and there was no way I was going through basic training again… I had no more weight to lose!

Near the end of basic training, I had a pass to go home for the weekend. We were in formation outside our barracks when my drill sergeant came up to me and said,

"Massaro, you have a pass to go home this weekend?"

"Yes, Drill Sergeant. I do."

"Let me see that pass."

I handed it to him, and he tore it up.

"What are you doing? I haven't been home in weeks."

"You came in second place in your inspection today."

"You have to be kidding!"

He wasn't. At this point, I was thinking about how glad I was to have been the one who knocked the gas mask out of his hand. He did not let me go home that weekend. It turned out that he didn't because he had duty that weekend and wanted me to be on duty with him. One night, he and I took a police Jeep and patrolled Columbia, South Carolina. Riots were going on, and he had to patrol the area. I was only a trainee, and I was not supposed to patrol anything, but that night the Sergeant put false stripes on my uniform to make it look like I was a patrol sergeant and told me to get in. He said to me, "When I get out of this Jeep, put your back up against my back and keep it there." He wanted little old untrained me to have his back. Thank God nothing happened.

The next night we played Monopoly for hours. Then, he took me home for dinner with him and his wife. We became friends and had respect for each other. On the last day of basic training, we had to run a confidence course. My drill sergeant said to me, "Massaro, lead your men through this confidence course and show them what confidence really is."

The first part of the course consisted of five telephone poles used as stairs to a platform to jump off into wood shavings. I ran up the telephone poles and tripped over the last one, did a head dive into the wood chips, and came up smiling. My drill sergeant said, "Men, don't follow Massaro." My nose was bleeding, and I had scrapes over my face, but that was the end of my basic training. I was done!

***

My wife and my parents received the following letter from the department of the Army while I was in basic training.

Joseph, as this date May 8, 1970, has been selected as an outstanding soldier of the first basic combat training brigade. Only soldiers who have clearly demonstrated outstanding leadership abilities are so chosen. This procedure is as old as the Army itself; the competition for the honor of being named an outstanding soldier is keen. Traditionally, this soldier is assigned a duty of special trust and honor. In this brigade, the outstanding soldier is interviewed by the brigade commander and discusses all aspects of basic combat training. Your son is to be commended for putting forth the considerable effort required to be designated as an outstanding soldier. I know you will be pleased to learn of this recognition that he has earned. A copy of this correspondence will be placed in your son's official file.

Sincerely,

ALBERT W. SMARR JR,

LIEUTENANT COLONEL

When I finished my basic training, I had new confidence in myself. I might have been a disaster in school, but I knew I would do well in life thanks to the United States National Guard. After basic training, Ronnie and I went to Fort Gordon, Georgia, for our radio relay training. For the next couple of months, we learned to set up antennas and radio equipment so the Army could have communications in the field. During the training, both Ronnie's and my wife flew down to Augusta, Georgia, for a weekend. It was the first time my wife ever flew in an airplane. She didn't like it then, and she doesn't like it now. At the end of that schooling, I came out of there with a hundred percent on every test. I think my mother owes me a few hundred dollars. The new duty was a lot easier than basic training. Ronnie and I had an air-conditioned room. Why? Because I was made temporary Sergeant again.

Every morning we assembled outside the barracks, and Sergeant Parish would come out to read the soldiers' names. Then, he would tell them what their next duty was. Now, if you remember, I've already mentioned that although we were enlisted in the National Guard, we trained along with the army recruits. We knew that when our training was over, we were going home.

Eighty-five percent of the guys we were standing with every morning were going to Vietnam! You could just see the looks on their faces as their names were called out, and the sergeant would say, "Republic of South Vietnam Charlie Land!" It was heartbreaking. I sure was lucky.

***

The first and second time I got drafted into the Army, I stepped up; I didn't complain. I took the oath and expected to go to Vietnam. It was a comedy of errors, pure luck that I was not one of them going to Vietnam. I'm not sure what would have happened to me over there, but whatever it was, it would not have been good. I saw what it did to my friend Eggplant's life. He had a bad case of post-traumatic stress syndrome. I was so happy to be going home and getting a chance to start where I left off. The Army had a way of tearing you down and building you back up. I remember when I first arrived at the reception center in Fort Jackson, South Carolina.

One day before we started our basic training, five guys came off the basic training hill; almost all of them had completed their training. These guys were so determined to go to Vietnam that we could not believe it. We thought they were just nuts. Most of the guys in our company who finished their basic training felt ready to go to war. I was happy to go through basic training. I was in the best shape of my life, and it gave me confidence in many areas. I surely am glad I didn't go to Vietnam, though; I would have gone if they sent me, but by some stroke of luck, I didn't have to, and I loved to tell a different story.

CHAPTER VI

Starting Again Sep. 1970

Before I left for my military training, we were still working in the old building in Elmsford. We had grown out of that building, and we had three draftsmen working in one small room. The shop's equipment was just hanging in the air and out of the way until it was needed. When I went back to work, the company moved to its new location in Peekskill, New York. The building they rented was about twice the size of the old building. I designed the new drafting offices and, of course, mine was the biggest. What did the company Elmsford Sheet metal look like in 1970? Up to this point, the company did small to medium size jobs. We had about twenty employees, and we were mainly fabricating and installing ductwork in houses and small office buildings.

***

Meet Pete D'Angules. He was the first employee. He started as a helper making ductwork with Vincent in his basement. They both would go out and install jobs. As the company grew, Pete became a draftsman, and he was very good at that job. When Pete drew the job, you knew everything was going to fit. Just before we moved to the new building, Pete was made manager of the company. Everybody liked Pete. He was a real nice guy. Both of Pete's sisters also worked there; Florence was the bookkeeper, and Ruth was the receptionist.

***

Meet Jack Mariando. He was the head draftsman. Jack had experience in handling larger jobs, and he was very talented. He was my immediate boss. Jack was a nice but sarcastic guy. If I made a mistake, he would let me know and make me mad, but this was good because it made me work harder. Now that I think of it, that's probably why he did it. Life was good. I had a job that was beyond my expectation. I was married to my beautiful high school sweetheart, we were living in our new house, which was only a twelve-mile drive from my shop, and we were happy. Some of the jobs required me to go to the field to do the measuring. I remember I was on my way to one job, and my uncle Vincent was taking my grandfather (his father) to the same job to show him the kind of work we were doing. When my grandfather saw me with the plans under my arm, he said to Vincent, "Look at my grandson the architect."

I wasn't actually an architect. I was a sheet metal draftsman, nowadays better known as a sketcher. My job was to create a complete set of fabrication and installation drawings for the sheet metal ductwork going into a building. The shop drawings would consist of the structural steel, the architectural walls, and the ceiling pattern, including the lights and air outlets. To accomplish this, the draftsman was given a complete set of drawings from the architect, including structural steel, piping and plumbing, fire protection, electrical and ductwork drawings. When the sketcher completed his drawings, he would have to submit them back to the engineer for approval.

When the drawings got back from approval, which could take a couple of weeks, there would often be changes requested from the engineer that would have to be updated. After this last step was completed, he would have to coordinate our work with the other trades to ensure there were no conflicts in the field. All the other trades would then coordinate with the sketcher who would need to prepare his drawing for fabrication. This would consist of breaking the sections of ductwork into individual pieces and then numbering each piece with a circle and a number in it. We would then transfer each piece to paper with all the information about that piece of duct on it so the shop could fabricate it and ship it to the right job.

There could be hundreds of pieces of ductwork on a drawing. All of this work had to be completed before we could start the job. We were a subcontractor, which means the owner of the building hired a general contractor. The general contractor would then go out and hire the different subcontractors to do the work. He would get bids from electrical and mechanical contractors. The low bid would get the job. The mechanical contractor was responsible for the plumbing and piping, fire protection, and the sheet metal. After he was awarded the job, he would go out to the different subcontractors to find the lowest price. This process could take a while, and by the time we were awarded the job, we were already late. It put a lot of pressure on the sketcher to get the drawings completed as fast as possible. Back in the 1970s, a sketcher used a pencil, a T-square, and a scale ruler to complete his work.

As I settled into my career, I noticed some old drafting methods that needed to be updated. For instance, we were drawing with regular type pencils that needed to be sharpened very often. I started using an automatic pencil that never needed to be sharpened. Pretty soon, the other sketchers were using that type of pencil too. I wanted to make a change to the way we created the shop ticket for the ductwork as well. Back then, if you wanted a radius elbow, you took your compass and drew the radius elbow on your plane paper pad. That was the way all the fittings were being put on shop tickets.

I came up with a pre-printed shop ticket with different shapes and fittings; all I had to do was fill out the sizes, piece number, and job number. I also noticed that each sketcher had a pad that he used for mathematics to establish the top and the bottom elevation of the duct. I came up with a three-wheel disc similar to a slide rule that eliminated doing the math. Numbering the individual pieces on the drawing was also time-consuming and hard to see after the drawings were printed. I came up with a Bates numbering system like the one used in grocery stores. Not only was it a lot faster, but the numbers on the drawings were a lot clearer, and you did not have to draw circles. Over the next couple of years, I came up with a few more time-saving ideas. I realize you probably don't know what most of these items are, but they helped us have the most productive drafting department in the sheet metal industry.

* * *

April 13, 1972, my daughter, Donna, was born. My wife became a stay-at-home mom. We had friends over the house almost every weekend. A Typical blue collar household with a vegetable garden in the backyard. My working hours were from 6 a.m. to 3:30 p.m., Monday through Friday. I worked most Saturdays from 6 a.m. to 12 p.m. I was getting good reviews from the sheet metal workers in the field installing my drawings. One weekend a month, I was going to my National Guard meetings. I moved up in rank to sergeant in charge of 20 men. We trained on radio relay equipment and set up antennas to broadcast the signals. My friend Ronnie was doing the same thing in his unit. We would go away for two weeks together for summer training while our wives would spend those two weeks together with our daughters. Ronnie and his wife had a daughter just before Donna was born. I was still going to the Adirondacks for the deer-hunting season every Thanksgiving. Monday nights, I picked up a bowling league with my friends. Everything seemed to be falling in place. I was truly living the American Dream.

CHAPTER VII

You Want Me To Do What?

The year was 1973. By now, my Uncle Vincent had turned over the company's day-to-day operations to Pete. Vincent spent most of his time with the Sheet Metal and Air Conditioning Contractors National Association (SMACNA). He would sit on several boards, including the National Joint Adjustment Board for the sheet metal industry. The committee's job was to resolve conflicts between the contractors and the Union Nationwide to avoid strikes. He got involved in any large bids our company made and played a lot of golf.

That year, for my two weeks of summer training with the National Guard, I applied for noncommissioned officer school at Camp Smith in the same town my shop was. *If I get this, it will keep me close to home and not sleeping in a tent,* I thought. I was accepted.

The second week of my training, my cousin showed up at the fort and said, "You have to call your uncle Vincent right away!"

"What's the matter?"

"I don't know, just call him."

I called my uncle Vincent that night and asked him what was going on. He told me he fired Pete, and I was the new manager, partner, and vice president. I think it took me a few minutes before I could breathe again.

Finally, I said to him, "Vincent… Are you crazy? I'm not qualified for that job and I don't want it. Don't do anything until I get back. I have a couple more days here. Promise me you won't do anything until I get back." He agreed to wait until I was finished with my training. I couldn't sleep that night. I was very content with what I was doing, and I knew I wasn't qualified for that position. I still had trouble writing letters, and now he wanted me to run a company.

A few days later, I finished with my training, and I walked into the office. I could immediately see that Vincent did not keep his promise. Pete's sister, the receptionist, was not a happy person. I walked into Vincent's office and sat down. I said,

"What the hell happened?"

"We had an opportunity to bid on the IBM (International Business Machine) World Trade Center in Tarrytown, New York. It would have been the biggest job we have ever bid on. Pete and I worked on the estimate together. We came up with a million dollar number which we knew would be tight. We knew our number would be good because no other local contractor could do the job. It would be too big for them. While I was away, Pete went to a meeting and dropped the number by 75,000 dollars. He didn't check with me first. We both knew that it was probably below our cost. I didn't think we would make any money on it and we have no choice now but to do it."

"Vincent, I don't want this job. I know absolutely nothing about the business end. I wouldn't know where to start. I am very happy with what I am doing. Why don't we keep Pete as a manager and then you can start training me on the business end?"

His mind was made up, and he was stubborn. I told him I was not interested in the job. We went back and forth for a while, and we finally agreed that we would keep Pete on and train me for the position. We called Pete into the office and told him the plan. He agreed and then quit later that night. I was too naïve to realize Pete could not stay there any longer. I gave him a hug when he left, thanking him for all that he had taught me. Not only did I say goodbye to Pete that day, but I also said goodbye to my comfortable life. I took my name plaque off of my office wall and put it on Pete's office door. When Vincent saw that, he said to me.

"You don't waste any time, do you?"

"I have no choice, you gave me the job. You, me and everyone who knows me will be concerned about your mental brain fart. Now, I have to figure out how to do this job!"

CHAPTER VIII

Now, Where Do I Start?

The very first night in my new position, after everybody left the shop, I sat in my new office wondering what the hell happened. I went over the list (in my mind) of what skills would be required to run a successful contracting business: Accounting and budgeting, negotiations, leadership, banking, collections, hiring and managing employees, project planning and execution, delegate, team building, sales and marketing, general manager's knowledge, spelling and letter writing. I didn't have any of the skills I was listing in my head and my uncle knew that! Did he just make one of the biggest mistakes of his career?

The following day, I was at work at 6 o'clock. I was going to wait for Vincent before we went and talked with everybody in the office. Nobody in the company knew that Pete quit the night before or that I was taking his place. I started going through some of the estimating files that Pete had for different jobs. At that stage, I had no idea how to price a job. I took the file folders and wrote all the different items down in that folder and then put the different prices Pete had on different jobs alongside each item. When Vincent came in, he asked me what I was doing, and I showed him the file folder with all the different items and pricing. He smiled and said, "You will do just fine, Joseph."

We called a meeting with everybody that was in the shop and the office. When Vincent told them that Pete quit and that I was the new General Manager, Vice President, and Partner, they were just as shocked as I was. Vincent and I met in his office to come up with the immediate priorities. A lot of the guys who now worked for me were old friends of mine. We would go bowling, fishing, hunting, drinking, etc., on a regular basis. Hell, I had grown up with some of those guys! One of the first things Vincent said to me was,

"You can't be friends with the people who work for you."

I said, "You want to bet?"

Most of them stayed with me until retirement.

The other thing he wanted me to do was to drop my union card. He explained that I was now management and I didn't need it anymore. I did what he suggested. As I look back on that decision today, I realize it was very foolish of me and very unfair of him. I could've kept that card being a worker/owner, and if I had, I would've benefited from the retirement plan the union offers. One might call Vincent 'Penny wise and dollar foolish.' Vincent's point was: if you save a quarter on an operation hundreds of times; eventually, it would lead to significant savings. So, he was cheap with the pennies but still spent thousands on his fancy cars. He did not want to pay the fringe benefits for me to stay in the Union, so he convinced me that I didn't need it. Was there another reason for him doing this besides the money? I don't know. All I know is thank God I was successful; today, all my men would be getting big pensions, and I would be living off social security.

When you were a business owner, being cheap is a helpful trait when used properly. For instance, most shops wrote all the information about the ductwork on the inside of the duct. That meant the men in the shop and on the job site would have to walk up to each piece of duct and look inside to see what the piece number and the job number were. This may sound trivial, but when we are looking at hundreds of fittings on a job site—where they are moving these fittings up and down the scaffolding to put into place —it actually takes up a lot of time to walk over and look inside a piece of ductwork. Vincent would have the shop guys write the information on the outside of the duct so you could see it from across the room. Most of this duct was buried inside the ceiling, so it didn't make any difference that the information was on the outside of the duct, except that it saved a ton of time for the guys installing it. Most shops worked off of a four-by-eight sheet of metal.

Vincent, with help from his neighbor, the machinist, built a coil line that could hold large coils of sheet metal. They also built a roller system and a shearing system; it allowed Vincent to introduce a new blanking system for the layout of sheet metal fittings which increased productivity from ten fittings a day per man to 35. It also reduced waste. If you needed an 85-inch piece, that's what you would cut off the coil line. Vincent used to say, "The scrap is still on the coil." So being frugal with the business end was a good thing, but being frugal with employees was a different story.

There were some controversial changes I wanted to make in the company. We had a contract negotiated between the contractors and the union, and I wanted to run this company by using that contract. We had people working on Saturdays and two hours a day for straight time when the contract called for overtime to be at double time. This limited who we could hire in the shop. The other thing was that some men were getting extra money per day. Some would get two dollars extra, some would get three dollars, and some would get none. The guy getting two dollars wanted to know why they were not getting three dollars.

I eliminated these problems and ran the company from the union contract. If you were a foreman, you got foreman pay. If you were a general foreman, that's how you were paid. If we needed you to work overtime, you got the overtime pay. This was not an easy change to make, but I figured I'd do it when everybody was in total shock about what happened with Pete. I wanted my outside foremen to come into a meeting to go over the jobs after work on

Thursday nights. These were union guys; it was unheard of for them to come in after work. I asked Pete, my old foreman, if he would come to my meeting; the other men respected Pete, and if I could get Pete to come, the other guys would follow. Pete was not very happy about it, but he would do it for me. All of the men agreed to the meetings, which really helped me out.

***

I started looking into jobs that were completed, comparing the contract price with a completed cost price. I went back about three years and started making a list. Most of the research I did was after hours, which my wife didn't love, but she knew I was just trying to get up to speed. When my list was completed, I noticed there was no consistency between profitable jobs and jobs that cost us money. Some jobs would make us five percent profit while others would make a ten percent profit, and some jobs lost ten percent out of pocket. There didn't seem to be rhyme or reason for any of it. I put the jobs that lost money on my list in red. They were very noticeable. I knew if I could figure out why these jobs went bad and not take that type of job in the future, we would be in much better financial shape. I met with Vincent to discuss job costing. We knew that the IBM job was going to be a stepping stone. If we did well on that job, it would open doors to other jobs of this size. Through this research and my meeting with Vincent, I found out that we had absolutely no job costing. We had no way of knowing what our products really cost, and we didn't have the equipment in the shop that we needed to handle that size job. The IBM job was at least three times bigger than any other job we had thus far. We had some work to do.

One summer, before I worked there, Vincent hired my brother 'The Genius' to do some time studies to come up with any kind of job costing; they did not come up with anything. Vincent knew the business well. He was an intelligent guy, and he was always trying to improve productivity in his shop. When I told him we needed to figure out the job cost, he was all for it. There was a show coming up in Las Vegas for contractors where we could see all the latest equipment available in the industry. Vincent booked the trip for him and me to go to Las Vegas and see what was new. At the end of our meeting, Vincent said that we had to do a layoff, and we were not quite ready to hit the IBM job hard. He explained that since I was new there, he would do the layoffs. I said, "No, Vincent, it's my job and I'll do the layoffs." It was my first time laying people off. I told them they would be coming back as soon as we got things going on the IBM job and that we were planning on taking bigger jobs to keep all the guys working full-time. I did all the layoffs myself for years. One mechanic once told me I was the only boss who laid him off with dignity.

CHAPTER IX
Vegas Baby 9

Vincent and I were on our final descent into Las Vegas when he turned to me and said, "Joe, when we're in Las Vegas don't ask me to borrow money. I will not lend you money in the casino. When we are on the plane going out of Vegas, if you need money, I'll be glad to lend it to you. But that's my hard fast rule." Vincent and I went to Las Vegas many times over the years. Every time we started to descend, he would give me that same speech. We stayed in Caesars Palace on our first trip, and it was the first casino I had ever been in. Coming from what we thought was a luxury vacation in the Adirondacks at our little camp with no electricity or running water, you can only imagine the culture shock when I walked into that over-the-top casino/hotel.

We went out for a nice dinner every night in a fancy restaurant, and then we spent some time gambling at the casino. What I was really looking forward to was the sheet metal show the next day. As we walked into the show the next morning, Vincent said to me, "This show is so big that we're going to spend the whole day just walking down every aisle and taking notes on what we want to see tomorrow." He was right. The show was huge, but only about 20 percent of it would be interesting to us. That night, we had dinner

and talked about what we had seen that day. The next day, we
headed directly to the Lockformer Company.

The company was dedicated to the sheet metal industry. They
built many types of equipment for our industry. Our local
distributor for Lockformer was a friend of Vincent; he was at the
show, and that's who we met. The machine I was most interested in
was called a 'Welty Way'. It was used to make standard lengths of
duct ten times faster than we could make it. This type of ductwork
was used in 60 percent of every job. If we wanted to do larger jobs,
this piece of equipment would be necessary. We would also need
the equipment to keep up with the IBM job we already had on the
books. We made arrangements for the salesmen to meet us at our
office the following week. Vincent and I spent the next couple of
days looking at other types of equipment and playing some
blackjack at night. I was playing two-dollar blackjack, and Vincent
was playing five-dollar blackjack. Because of the different boards
Vincent sat on in our industry, he knew people from all over the
country. We had dinner and drinks with all different kinds of
people. It was definitely a lifestyle I wasn't used to living.

The following week we met with the salesman from
Lockformer. This one machine was going to cost us 80,000 dollars.
We didn't have much of a choice—we needed the machine to get
the IBM job done. We ordered the machine on the spot, and we had
to find a way to pay for it. I was shocked after all the years in

business, the company did not have 80,000 dollars. *He hardly has any money in this company,* I thought. Vincent lived in a nice house, always had a brand-new big car, and belonged to a country club. Where the hell was all the money?

What did I get myself into? Actually, a more accurate question was… what did he get me into? I remember one time my father came home and said to my mother, "Your big shot brother was in today. I had to lend him the money to make his payroll, again." Vincent was from the depression years. He learned to spend his money as fast as he could make it. For him, it was okay, but for the business… not so much.

CHAPTER X

Rebuilding On A Shaky Foundation With An Unskilled Laborer, Me

What do you think the Vegas odds would be on this company surviving? I've been known to go all-in on number 27 in roulette. Talk about your long shot!

Our priority in my new vice president position was the IBM job. We had not signed the contract yet. The first thing we needed to do on this project was to submit our duct construction standards to the engineer. As I looked into the specifications for this job, I immediately found a conflict with the type of connectors they wanted to use on the project. The connectors specified were used primarily for high-velocity ductwork, which the job was not requiring. If we were forced to use these connectors on this project, we would go broke. We called for a meeting with IBM and the engineers to clarify the connectors.

At that meeting, the engineer insisted that the connectors were the ones he wanted on this project. We told IBM that if that was the case, we couldn't take the project. After a couple more meetings with IBM and the engineer, we resolved the problem using the standard type connectors for that type of duct. We signed the contract, and I took the lead on the job. After we signed, I swung by my mother's house to tell her the good news. I walked in and said, "Hey, Ma, guess what your dumb kid did today? I landed our biggest job yet."

***

The building was already up, and we were already late. I put the other sketches on the IBM project and started drafting a drawing myself to get the job underway. As I studied the drawings, I became aware that the building was split into two identical wings. I needed to come up with a way of drawing only one wing and then making a mirror image of that wing. It would cut our drafting cost in almost half and help to get the job back on schedule. The way we accomplished this was by making a drawing of the ductwork without any writing on it. When that was finished, we printed it upside down on a mylar and then added the text to both drawings. Every week at the job meeting, they asked me where the ductwork for the job was. After a couple of weeks, we finally started getting some ductwork for the project out the door. I told my truck driver that when he came in with the first load of duct, to stop in front of the trailer where we were having our meeting and blow the horn, they would notice our truck full of ductwork. He would then drive back out of the job site without unloading the truck and finally returning 15 minutes later and doing it again. That way, they would think that we were bringing several truckloads of duct, and they would eventually get off my back about it.

The IBM drawings were coming along. We had some ductwork on the job being installed. The top priority was sitting down with the bank to establish a line of credit so we'd have money for machinery and payroll. We were also going to need to hire a new bookkeeper and a receptionist. To no one's surprise, Pete's sisters quit shortly after he left. One other priority was to change our accountants. We were going to need certified statements in order to borrow the amount of money we would need to build the company.

We schedule a meeting with the bank that Vincent had been working with for many years. We brought the signed contract with us for the IBM job, along with the purchase order on the Welty Way. We were looking for a 500 thousand dollar line of credit, but we ended up with a 300,00 dollar line of credit secured with our houses. I had to get my wife to sign the loan documents. That was not an easy job; it was a big risk to put our house on the line.

Let's take a look at what a sheet metal construction company has to go through to take a job from bid to finish: 95 percent of the work we got we had to bid on. Most of the time, we had to be the low bidder to win the job. We had to bid approximately ten jobs to win just one. Some of these jobs took a couple of weeks to do the takeoff and the pricing. We had no job cost information on previous jobs, so we were not really estimating… we were guesstimating. Once we would sign a contract for a job, we would get zero money upfront. We had to produce the sheet metal drawings without getting paid. Next, we had to purchase the material and fabricate the ductwork. We couldn't get paid for the ductwork until it was installed on the job. Once we installed ductwork at the end of that month, we could finally submit a bill. The bill was based on the percentage of completion of the job. I had to personally walk the job with the construction manager, prove the percentage complete, then argue about it.

Thirty days after we submitted our bill, they paid 90 percent of it. They held back ten percent as a retainer just in case anything went wrong. Since we were a third-tier subcontractor, we were last to get paid. Why would anybody be in this business? We had hundreds of thousands of dollars laid out. It was almost like a self-inflicted Ponzi scheme. You had to continuously use the money from the jobs that were running in order to start new jobs. The average profit for mechanical contractors was two percent. Of course, I knew none of this when he made me his partner. The only thing I could do was take it one step at a time and see how far I could get.

The most important thing I needed to do at the beginning was to start some cash flow. That hundred thousand dollar job that we had was in fabrication. I offered them a discount if they would prepay, and they took it. I met with IBM and talked to them about paying us some money for the drafting and fabrication of the duct. That would give us a little breathing room. The next step was setting up the new equipment that just came in. For any new equipment that we put in the shop, I would personally supervise the installation and the operation. I knew every piece of my shop equipment inside and out. Next, we invited the top IBM construction executive to visit our shop. He was so impressed watching the men layout fittings that he called them 'Real Craftsmen'.

After seeing our shop in action, he had no problem giving us the money we asked for. His name was Mayo Borman. Over the years, he and I became friends. I did many jobs for IBM. If I had a problem on any IBM job, all I had to do was call Mayo, except one time when he was close to retirement. I called him with a problem I had on a large IBM job. He said, "Joe leave me alone. I'm too close to retirement. Over the years you've talked me into doing too many things I should not have done." He couldn't help himself, though; he really liked me, so he helped anyway.

Next, I had to hire a new secretary and a new bookkeeper. I never interviewed anybody for a job before, nor had I ever been interviewed; it was complete on-the-job training for me. I hired a new secretary, a new bookkeeper, and a new estimator. His name was Ralph Jacobs, and he was 75 years old. Ralph knew the construction business well. I also hired a new accountant that could produce certified statements for us, which we would need to grow even bigger. The IBM World Trade Headquarters job was going well; it was their world trade center. It was a V-shaped building with typical mirror wings. This building design saved us a lot of time and money. It was a busy time for the construction industry, and there was a lot of work available.

We started bidding on several projects. One project was a large hospital in our area. We were asked to bid by Kirby Saunders, a large mechanical contractor out of New York City. We were invited down to their office to go over the job. We went through a checklist to make sure we had everything covered. Steve Cole, who was the main buyer for Kirby Saunders, knew Vincent. He said, "Vincent you have to make your number lower or I can't give you the job." Vincent asked him if he had a set of drawings and an office we could use to see if there was any way we could get some money off. Steve said, "No problem," and gave us a set of drawings and an office. Vincent and I walked into that office and shut the door.

I went to open up the drawings when Vince asked, "What are you doing?"

"I'm opening the drawings up to see where we can save money."

"Don't bother, we are taking the job at their number. I just don't want them to know how easily I dropped the price."

Another lesson learned; never show the other guy your hand in the card game.

***

We won several more jobs that year. We were running out of room in the shop we were renting. We heard of a building coming up for sale in the same town: Peekskill, N.Y. The building was originally a sheet metal shop,s that was perfect. Vincent knew the guy who was selling it; his name was Phil Miller. The building would've been perfect for us. It was on five acres of land, which was plenty of room for expansion. We went to the building to check it out and met with Phil in his office. Vincent asked him how much he was asking for the building. Phil told us the price was 250,000 dollars. We told Phil we would get back to him. Vincent asked me if I noticed that Phil was the only person in the entire building. They were in big trouble. It could've been a great deal for us. Two hundred fifty thousand dollars was a lot of money in 1975. I was in Vincent's office when he called Phil and told him that we would give him 180,000 for the building. Phil said,

"You are crazy."

"That's my offer. If you call me back, that's the offer that you take or don't call me back," Vincent responded.

Phil called 15 minutes later and said he would go to 225,000.

"Phil, I told you don't call me back unless you would take 180,000."

Phil then called back and said he would go to 200,000. Vincent told Phil not to call him anymore. Phil called back again and said his best number was 195,000. Vince said, "I told you not to call me," and hung up on him. He turned to me and said, "We just bought a building."

"What are you talking about? He said 195,000 was the best number," I said.

"Once he went below 200,000 we had him."

Phil called and sold us the building for 180,000 dollars. Vincent said to me,

"We need a 15,000 dollar deposit."

"Okay, I'll get you a check for 7,500."

"No, you have to do the whole 15,000. I don't have the cash right now."

Another lesson learned...Vincent never had cash when we were buying something big.

***

One time, we were in Lake Tahoe with our wives. It was late, so I was on my way to bed. Vincent was still sitting at a blackjack table with hundreds of dollars in chips in front of him. The following day, I went down through the casino to get breakfast, and he was still sitting at the same table, except for this time he had no chips in front of him. As he finally got up to go to his room, he saw me and came rushing over to ask me to lend him a couple of hundred dollars. I said,

"Vincent, I'm sorry but we're in a casino, and I can't lend you any money."

He got so mad and started yelling, "I don't want money for gambling, I just want some pocket money!"

"Sorry, Vincent, that's what they all say," and I walked away. I waited a long time for that.

On September 25, 1974, my youngest daughter Jennifer was born. I now had two beautiful daughters, a beautiful wife, the house I always wanted, and a business I never wanted. None of us realized what the real cost of successes or failures was going to be. The time I had to put into learning how to run a company was time away from my family. I tried to make it to all their school plays. I made most of them. One time, the teacher asked my daughter Donna to draw a picture of her father. She drew a picture of me working. The hours I had to put in were stressful for everybody. There always seemed to be a crisis at work. Even when I was home, my mind was someplace else.

CHAPTER XI

Moving On Up

I was finally beginning to get the hang of the running-a-business thing. I had done a lot of work on our cost analysis, which had never been done in our office before. I was beginning to understand how to bid on our jobs. Vincent and I worked on our next project bid together and came up with a reasonable number. Vincent was going away on a business trip, and he left the negotiations of this project to me. He told me not to go below 75,000 dollars. When he came back into my office later that week, he asked,

"Did we get the job?"

"Of course we got the job."

"Did you get 80,000 dollars?"

"No."

"Did you get 70,000 dollars?"

"No, I didn't get 70,000 dollars."

"Did you get 75,000 dollars?"

"No, I didn't get s 75,000 dollars."

"What the hell did you get then? I told you not to go below s 75,000 dollars!" He yelled.

I looked at him, smiled, and calmly said, "Vincent, I got 101,000 dollars for the job."

He didn't believe me. He said, "I know you're always making jokes, but this isn't the time to make jokes, Joseph, this is business."

I took the purchase order out of my desk and slid it across to him. He looked at that purchase order; he looked at me, smiled, and left my office.

On my way home that night, I swung by my mother's house to tell her the good news. I walked in and said, "Hey, Ma, guess what your dumb kid did today? I landed a job for 26,000 dollars more than Vince wanted for it!"

The business was really starting to pick up by this point. Not the greatest time to move the shop, but we had already purchased the new building, so we had to do it. We had six years left on the original lease of our existing building. Luckily, we found somebody to sublease it from us. The first thing I needed to do to prepare for the move was to lay out the new shop where all the equipment would be placed. That was a job I could only do after hours because I was so busy trying to keep the place running. First, I measured the new shop. Then I measured every piece of equipment that we had. I made a drawing of every piece of equipment to scale, then cut them out and placed them on my drawings of the new shop. When I was satisfied with the layout, I spray painted the new shop floors where each piece of equipment was to go. That way, when the equipment was delivered, it could be put right in the space where it belonged. The workflow was critical; you wanted the raw materials to come in one door and the finished products to go out the other. We were always looking for ways to reduce bottlenecks. We could not afford to lose any fabrication time because of this move.

Vincent, myself, and my shop foreman, Frank Sunda, put a plan together. Vincent always said, "Even a bad plan is better than no plan." Over the next couple of days, we precut a lot of metal so that when we started in the new shop, we could be ready to fabricate immediately. On the Friday of our move, we shut down the old shop at 3:30 p.m. and started moving equipment immediately. The following Monday morning, we started back working on duct for our current job at the new shop. The equipment we needed immediately was up and running, and the rest of it was being worked on. The new shop was only about five miles from the old shop. It was a round-the-clock operation that went very smoothly. The last piece out of the old shop was the large fork truck. I had to drive it the last five miles because it was too heavy to put on the truck.

The new shop was perfect for us. Elmsford Sheet Metal and Westchester Air Conditioning were up and running. The only problem was that we didn't have enough time or money to hardwire the equipment. We kept it up and running with a temporary system, so we didn't disrupt our busy workflow. We had the coil line running well, but when I went out to the shop, I saw two men running the coil line instead of the usual one guy. When I asked them why they needed two guys, they told me the machine was so fast that one man couldn't run the machine and label the duct with a magic marker. I needed to give it some thought. Do you remember my first day when I told you I listed all the costs for the completed job we did that year? Many of the jobs were in the red, meaning we lost money on them. I analyzed these jobs until I found out why they went bad. It turned out we were not charging enough for a small duct. Any duct under 12 by 12 was being charged at four pounds a running foot. A 24 by 24 piece of duct would cost the same amount of money to fabricate and install as a 12 by 12 piece of duct. I came up with a simple formula to prevent us from taking bad jobs until I had solid job costing information. I took the footage ductwork and the total amount of weight divided by the amount of footage by the weight to get an average weight per foot. If it was over ten pounds per foot, it was an okay job. Anything under ten pounds, my competitors could have it.

I set up a meeting with IBM to look at their computer and a meeting with Burroughs Corporation to see what they had. They both had a computer that would help us with payroll and job costing. Computers were new at this time, but if they would save us money and manpower, it could've been worth the investment. IBM came in with a price of 32,000 dollars. Burroughs came in with a price of 28,000 dollars. There was no way I was getting Vincent to go for that kind of money.

***

Meet Lonnie Brinker. Lonnie was the salesman for the Burroughs Corporation. He went over all the capabilities of the computer and how the payroll was done. The job cost would've been a byproduct of the payroll. I liked what I saw, but I told Lonnie there was no way I could go for 28,000 dollars. He asked to make him an offer. I talked with Vincent, and he said to offer him 18,000 dollars. I figured that was a good way to get rid of him, but Lonnie took the offer to my surprise. As a matter of fact, it's been about 50 years, and I still haven't gotten rid of Lonnie; he turned out to be one of my best friends!

The computer was delivered about a week later and set up by the technician to ensure it was running right. I bought the computer with a contractor's package. At 5 o'clock that night, Lonnie showed up, and we installed the software. We worked about three hours the first night, but we didn't get too far. We could get the programs to work up to a certain point, but when we tried to use the job costing feature, the computer would fail. We did this for about four nights.

Towards the end of the fourth night, I said to Lonnie, "You don't know what the hell you're doing, do you?" He then told me that it was the first contracting package he ever tried installing. I said, "Let's go have a beer, we will figure it out."

The next day Lonnie called me and said his boss was taking him off the project. I told Lonnie to get his boss on the phone; I had just found someone I could work well with, I wasn't letting him go that easily. The next day, Lonnie was back. He talked to someone else who installed the contracting package in the South. They told him the number they had us enter into the computer was wrong. We tried the new number he gave us, and the system finally came to life.

We hired three part-time secretaries; they were all friends of each other; Mary, Alice, and Rose. They were perfect for what we needed. We trained Mary on the computer for payroll and job costing, while Alice and Rose answered the phones, typed letters, and kept the office organized. We developed a new time slip with all the different work items on it so we can start developing job costing.

My next project was to work on a way to mark the ductwork coming off my coil line automatically. The coil line was running so fast that the guys couldn't keep up with it. I started working on a printing system that would stamp the numbers on the bottom of the duct. I got this system to work, but I couldn't get the ink to stick to the ductwork. I noticed that the computer I bought for 18,000 was sitting idle four days a week because its only job was payroll and job cost. I called Lonnie, my computer salesman, and asked him what else the computer could do. He told me it could do whatever I programmed it to do! I came up with an idea. Why not have the computer produce a label that could be stuck on each piece of duct?

The shop tickets were sent to the shop foreman to figure out the blanking size for each piece of duct. He used a book to tell the true lengths of certain fittings. It took him several hours each day, but the computer could do these things using mathematics. I put together a specification for each type of fitting that we used.

I called Lonnie and asked him if he knew a programmer. He gave me the name of one in New York City. I picked him up at the train station later that week and showed him what I needed to be done. He asked me a few questions and said he'd be back in four weeks. Four weeks later, he returned to my office with a paper punch tape that contained the programming data for the labeling program. He entered it into the computer, and nothing happened. He said he had to make a few changes and would be back in a week. A week later, he was back in my office with another punch tape. This time, when he put it into the computer, a program showed up! I was impressed.

I entered the duct into the computer as it asked you questions, and the computer would produce a "stick on" label for every piece of metal going out of the shop. The label was a three-by-five sticker containing the job name, number, and type of fitting with a picture of what the fitting looked like and the blanking size required to make it. The 18,000 dollar investment in the computer was starting to pay off big time. My coil line went from a two-man operation to a one-man operation. My high-priced draftsmen were spending 25 percent more time on drawings instead of taking off fittings. I had an apprentice doing all the pickoff work right into the computer. My shop foreman could spend all his time running the shop. The program also produced a shipping list so we could be sure each piece got to the job.

Over the next couple of months, I refined the printing of the label to be color-coded. Sometimes, five different jobs were running in the shop simultaneously, so with the color-coding system, we could easily see which job was which. We also added different colored stripes to the labels so we could not only define what floor on the job each piece would go to but what corner of that floor each piece would go. Around 40 percent of the insulation costs of ductwork were material handling. This system was saving us a ton of time.

By the end of 1974, we had landed four additional jobs. I swung by my mother's house with each new job we landed to tell her what her dumb kid was up to. Of course, she didn't think I was dumb, but after growing up with an aeronautical engineer for a brother and a lawyer for a sister, I guess I developed a little complex. But my mom was my biggest cheerleader. She loved sharing my success with me. Even after she died and I sold the company, I took the check to the cemetery to show her. It was a bittersweet moment.

***

We were getting so much new work that we needed a bigger line of credit. Our new accountants had produced certified statements for us to bring to the Bank of New York. They turned us down. Our accountant recommended another bank named Manufacture Hanover which handled contractors. We sat down with them and showed them our growth pattern. We asked for a one million dollar line of credit. They approved us. We paid off the other bank and moved everything to Manufacture Hanover. With our new computer system in place, I could now see how our finances were tracking every month. We were doing a little better, but we were not setting the world on fire. With all the new changes in place, I started to build confidence with the people who worked for me and myself. With the new computerized system, I knew my competitors couldn't fabricate ductwork at a price I could. I decided we were going to form a sister company to sell fabricated ductwork to our competitors. We named the company East Coast Sheet Metal; that way, customers wouldn't buy ductwork directly from their competitor... at least they didn't know they were! I made a brochure showing the different fittings and the pricing for our fabricated duct and shared it with both union shops and non-union shops.

In 1975, the computer system was running so well that I wanted to see if it was marketable. There was a show coming up in January, the same type of show I purchased my Welty Way coil line at. This one was in Atlanta, Georgia. I called Lonnie, my computer salesman, and asked him if he thought we could get a couple of these computers to display at the show. These computers were nothing like today's little portable ones; they were so big they needed to be moved with a fork truck. He checked with his company, and they agreed to supply two computers for the show. I rented a booth, and Lonnie and I flew out to Atlanta to present at our first sheet metal show. The sheet metal industry was labor-intensive and antiquated. Contractors were looking for technology to help them stay competitive. It was a three-day show, and for three days, our booth was packed. Contractors were standing four rows deep, watching our demos. One older, southern gentleman came up to me after a demo and said, "Boy, I take my hat off to you!" That was a great compliment. We came out of that show with 350 leads. East Coast Sheetmetal not only fabricated duct but now, all of a sudden, we sold computerized equipment for the entire sheet metal industry.

In 1977 I got a telephone call from a Danish company. Their office was in New Rochelle, New York, about 20 miles from us.

He told me that their company worked around the world for the United States military. He asked me if I would bid on a job that he had in the Azores. The job consisted of ripping out all the ductwork in a small hospital due to the ductwork rusting and falling through the air outlets. He told me the price must've included somebody going to the site to measure the job and ship the ductwork to the Azores for his men to install. I gave them a price of 22,000 dollars. He gave me the job and set up a date for him and me to meet on site. My people wanted to know why I would go to the Azores for a 22,000 dollars job. It was only going to be a three or four-day trip, and I needed a break. The manager of the company was Bo Nealson.

We met at a temporary office he had in the Azores. They took me to the job site. I was going to measure up the job, but as I checked the job out, I found that the ductwork was not rusting. In fact, the rust came from the fans on the roof and then falling into the ductwork. I met with Mr. Nielsen and told him the situation. He said to me,

"Mr. Massaro, this is a government job, you can't change a government job."

"Mr. Nielsen, if we rip out all the ceilings and all the duct and you replace it, it's still going to rust. How is that going to make you look?"

"Mr. Massaro, I will set up a meeting with the Army Corps of Engineers tomorrow morning but we're going to lose the job."

That night, I sat in my room with a pack of Marlboros and a red pencil and made a little drawing of the situation. The next day, we met with the Army Corps of Engineers and a procurement officer, who was a southern boy, said to the general,

"Sir, this heir boy is from New York. He says your drawings are full of crap." Mr. Nielsen turned white! The general said to me,

"Did you say my drawings are full of crap?"

"No, sir, but there is a problem with them."

I had no place to put my drawing down, so I sat on the floor, and the general sat next to me. I explained the situation to him, and at the end of that explanation, I told him we could fix the problem without a contract change in price. He looked at me and said,

"I guess my drawers are full of crap, let's do it your way."

The color came back into Mr. Nielsen's face; we both just hit a home run. Mr. Nielsen didn't have to rip out the ceilings or the ductwork. All he had to do was replace the fans and clean the duct. We both made a very nice profit. From then on, we did jobs all around the world for him.

CHAPTER XII

Building Our Reputation

At the end of 1977, we had been doing most of the IBM jobs in our area. Our reputation with IBM was excellent. They knew we could complete their jobs on time and that we did quality work. We also picked up a large job in Cuba with Mr. Nielsen's Company. We were not only sketching and fabricating for him but now we were doing the installation on a job in Guantánamo Bay, Cuba. We also landed a very big job at the General Motors facility in Tarrytown, New York. We had a good reputation with this facility. Every job we have done at the plant, we brought in on time. That was important to them; when they wanted to push the button and start running their line, you needed to get out of their way. It was a very difficult job. It was on the roof in the middle of this huge building. It looked like we were going to need helicopters to remove the old equipment and ductwork and install the new work.

Helicopter work was very expensive and dangerous. Once we won the job, we sat down to review it to see where we could save money. On the GM job, I took Don Trier down to the job site. We went up on the roof where the job was to be done and started looking around. How could we get the material off the roof without using a helicopter? There was no clear path across the roof; we were absolutely in the middle of the building. On the roof was where they ran many of their ovens for curing the paint on the cars.

We went there on a Sunday because we knew the ovens would be off. On the roof, there were access doors to allow maintenance to the oven. We entered the oven where the job site was and started walking through the oven. Every time we came across another access door, we would open it to see where we were on the roof. When we opened the eighth door, to our surprise, it was overlooking the parking lot. It was the break we needed. We could set a crane in the parking lot and unload and load from that position. We disassembled everything in the middle of the building and used the ovens to move everything through the inside of the oven to the crane. Another successful job done.

***

We started to see a slowdown in the construction industry in the middle of 1978 all across the country. The forecasts were not good for the next two years with Jimmy Carter in the White House. My computer company, East Coast Sheetmetal, was still doing demos on the labeling system. The problem was that the computer was so big and heavy that we were not getting a lot of sales.

Lonnie called me one day and said he saw an advertisement that Radio Shack came out with a personal computer, and there was a show in my area the following night. Lonnie and I went to the show. Radio Shack was demonstrating computers they could pick up with their hands; mine needed a forklift. There was no way that a small computer could do the work that my big computer was doing. I brought a sample of the label that my computer was producing. Lonnie and I walked up to a guy working on one of the computers and showed him my label. We asked him if his computer could create a label like ours. He looked at the label and said yes. I asked how long it would take to program that into his computer. He looked at me and said, "Give me 15 minutes." Lonnie and I just looked at each other in disbelief. It took us months to get the label out of our computer, and this kid said he could have it done in 15 minutes. As promised, 15 minutes later, we were shocked; it worked. The next day, I looked for a programmer who could write a program for the Radio Shack computer.

Another HVAC (heating, ventilation, air conditioning) show came up in January in New Orleans, and I wanted to show our new, portable system there. The new system was far more advanced than the old labeling system. The old system would type the questions on a piece of paper, then you would need to type the answers in, and it had no screen to work from. The Radio Shack system had a screen to show the user a picture of the piece of duct he wanted to make. Then all it had to do was fill in the answers. I had Radio Shack in New Orleans provide the computers for my show. When my system was completed, we had a video of the computer system in every Radio Shack store in America. I sold two systems at the show that year: one to a contractor in Boston and one to a contractor in the Netherlands. When the system was completed, I flew out to the Netherlands to train the software users. The problem we had with training their workers was that they spoke Dutch and I spoke English. The only saving grace was that we both spoke sheet metal; we were able to work around the language barrier and get them trained.

In New Orleans, Vincent took me to the first shop he ever worked in. Whenever we traveled, we would stop to see other sheet metal shops. Vincent knew a lot of the owners from being connected with the Sheet Metal Contractors Association. We looked at much bigger sheet metal shops than ours. None of the shops we looked at were able to keep up with our productivity.

Work started slowing down badly in our area in 1979. There were not many jobs around, and we were fighting for every one of them. I still went upstate with the Hunters every Thanksgiving week like we had been doing since the camp was built. I had many good friends up there, one of which owned a pizza shop and knew a lot of people in Lake Placid.

CHAPTER XIII

If You Think You're In A Hole, Stop Digging

Meet Mike Nicole. The 1980 Winter Olympics were coming to Lake Placid, and the town was buzzing! The word on the street was that you couldn't buy a ticket for the Olympics. The Olympic Committee told the vendors they would stop selling tickets in August, five months before the Olympics started. The only way spectators could get a ticket would be through a vendor. Mike told me he had a friend who could get us as many tickets as we wanted if we became a vendor. I sat down with Vincent, and we started kicking some ideas around. *We may be able to make a lot of money as a vendor,* I thought. The idea was that we would need to provide a total package for the guest, including parking, housing, tickets, food, and transportation to the venue. It didn't seem like too much of a risk at the time.

Being an Olympic vendor was going to be a large undertaking. We needed to take this step-by-step. The first step was to find a place where we could house people. Most houses in Saranac and Lake Placid had been rented over five years before in anticipation of these events. This was our first big problem. Vincent and I went to Lake Placid to see what alternatives we could come up with. We looked at an old farmhouse about 20 miles from the Olympics headquarters, but it was too far. As we were driving around, we came across a campsite for trailers. We decided to meet with the owner, Henry. Henry was an older fella, and his campsite was perfect. It was ten miles from Lake Placid and only four miles from the downhill skiing events. There were about 40 campsites already on the site. We told Henry we wanted to rent his place during the Olympics. We would build 100 trailer sites which would include electricity and a water source for each trailer. Henry was interested, but he needed to talk to his family and would get back to us with a price.

The next piece of the puzzle: *where are we going to get 100 trailers?* It didn't take long to realize that we could not rent 100 trailers, so we set up a meeting with the Shasta Company. They made trailers. We talked to them about purchasing 124-foot trailers. We needed to know that they could build them and have them on the job site well before the Olympics were to start. They said they could. Henry got back to us and told us his family was willing to rent us the property for 40,000 dollars. Things were actually moving along pretty well.

The next major item was meeting with the Olympic Committee, presenting them with our plan, and seeing if they were willing to give us the tickets. We set the meeting up in Lake Placid a week later. They liked our plan and gave us a brochure of how the tickets would be sold. We couldn't just sell tickets to the best events; they had to be paired with other events. If we requested a skating ticket, we might have to take a biathlon ticket with it. They wanted to ensure that all events had ticket sales. We put a package together where people could rent a trailer for a two, three, or five-day package. They could pick what events they wanted and what dates they wanted to go. The buses would pick them up at the trailer park and take them to the events they had purchased. Each trailer would have running water, frozen TV dinners in the freezers, and a place to park the car.

The cost of the trailers, the rental of the trailer park, the construction cost to upgrade the trailer park, the cost of the bussing, food and paper goods, legal, and advertising came out to one million dollars. If we charged 475 dollars per day, per person, at an average of four people per trailer for sixteen days of the Olympics, we could've made three to four million dollars. The best part of the whole deal was that it would be over in sixteen days. The only way to get tickets to the 1980 Winter Olympics after August was through the vendors. The Olympic Committee guaranteed they would not sell tickets after that date. I could be off on my calculations by two-thirds and still come out ahead of the game. What could possibly go wrong?

All we needed to do now was to see if the new bank would lend us the money. Vincent and I sat down with the bank to go over our plan. What we didn't know was that the new bank was a sponsor of the 1980 Winter Olympics. Vincent mentioned to the president of the bank that I had a 100,00 dollar CD I would put up as collateral. A few years prior, I had invested 5,000 in my brother's company, which developed the floppy disk. He would have to write his own book if you want to hear that story, but the good news for me was that my 5,000 dollars had turned into 100,000 dollars. It was easy for Vincent to put *my* money in as collateral without offering any of his own money. I put up my 100,000 dollars because I believed in the project. I didn't know if it was a good reason or not, but the banker gave us the money, stupid banker. Everything was falling into place. Next, it was time to execute this plan. I hired a local lawyer out of Lake Placid.

***

Meet Charles Walsh. He became my go-to guy for everything that I legally needed. He also knew a lot of people in town and had many contacts. The first thing I wanted him to do was to prepare all the contracts we needed for the property rental: the Olympic Committee contract, any permits I needed, and for him to try to keep me out of trouble. That was going to be his toughest job. Setting up my priorities: produce a layout of the future trailer park showing the trailer locations, the electrical locations, and the different watering spots. Upgrade the shower and bathroom area at the campsite, check on what permits we needed, prepare bid documents, go out to bid, meet with the trailer manufacturer and go over the layout we want on each trailer. Then, make sure they were winterized for the weather we would have in Lake Placid. Finally, we would have to figure out the timing for each trailer's delivery to the site.

After, start looking for bus companies that could handle this type of project and get quotes from them. Start analyzing the Olympic schedule to see what events we could put together to offer as a package. Find an advertising company to help us produce the brochure and start advertising. Find products to fill the trailers with since they would be stocked with food, toiletries, and paper products.

***

Vince and I decided to form a new company named Arlo Tours. Over the next couple of months, I ran back and forth to Lake Placid to get the contract we needed signed. Most of our business was conducted and handled at the local bar in town at a place called "Cottage". We also worked at Charles' office, which was in town.

Even though the contracting business had slowed down, ESM still required my attention, and I had to oversee the writing of the software program for East Coast Sheet Metal. I had a computer show coming up simultaneously as the Olympics, and I needed to make arrangements for somebody else to attend that computer show. Vincent and I drove out to Pennsylvania to see how the trailers were coming along. It looked like there would be no problem getting the one hundred trailers to the job site on time. Back up to Lake Placid, we met with Charlie to execute the Olympic Committee contract on the tickets.

We bought a 350,000 dollar check to pay for the tickets. Charlie begged me not to give the money to these people. He knew this was going to go downhill. He told me, "Joe, you do not know how incompetent these people are." I wasn't one to listen. I was confident my plan was solid, so I signed the contract and turned over the check. Remember I told you one of Charlie's jobs was to keep me out of trouble?

We hired a contractor to start working on the trailer park. The town we were building in was Wilmington, New York. Before our project, this town had no requirements for building permits. We did have to deal with the Adirondack Park Agency (APA) for any trees we needed cut. Getting the certificate of occupancy was a real challenge. Every time we thought we were close, something came up. Charlie would say to me, "Well, what are we going to do now?" And I would say, "Charlie, we go to plan B." We would come up with an alternate plan and go back with it to the APA, but some other problem would arise. Charlie would say, "Well we're stuck again, Joe, what are we going to do now?" I would tell Charlie, "We're going to go to plan C."

We were constantly changing our plan in every meeting we had to satisfy different people. The work on the trailer park was getting dragged out. If we could not get the park open, everything else would fall apart. We finally got everything ready for a final inspection. The electrical passed inspection, the water system passed inspection, the new showers we built passed inspection. The only thing left was approval by the fire department. At our final meeting with APA and the fire department, they announced for the first time that the corners on the roads were too narrow. They said they could not fit a fire truck through in case of an emergency. The Adirondack Park agency told us we could not cut any more trees. Charlie was ready to cut our losses and said,

"Joe, we made a good run of it, I think this is the end." There was no way I was quitting after all of this work. I told Charlie,

"We're going to plan in ZZ."

"What the hell is plan ZZ, Joe?"

"I'll tell you tomorrow."

Charlie and I left the meeting. I made a call back to my office to talk to my shop foreman, Frank Suda. I told him that I needed four guys and two chainsaws that night. That night the "A-Team" arrived. They cut the trees in question down to the dirt and then painted the stumps black. The next day we asked the fire department to take one more run-through to make sure they couldn't get their trucks to fit. They came back that day and drove the fire truck through the park; it was tight, but they made it. I had Charlie call for another meeting with the state and the fire department. At that meeting, the fire department announced that they could get the truck through. The Adirondack Park agency accused me of cutting more trees. I denied the allegation, and they said they had aerial photos of us cutting the trees. Charlie kicked me under the table and whispered, "You beat them."

"How is that, Charlie?" I said.

"By the time they find the aerial photos the Olympics will be over."

New York State issued us our certification of occupancy, and we were on our way. The project was on track! Everything that needed to be done up to this point had been done. We were spending a lot of money very quickly. The brochures for all the events were completed, and we were starting to advertise. My biggest concern was that the advertisement we put out had not produced any leads. Everybody I talked to said it was too early. People needed snow before they would start thinking about the winter Olympics. I hoped they were right, but for the first time in this adventure, I didn't have a warm and fuzzy feeling.

The first sign of trouble was when the United States boycotted the 1980 summer Olympics in Moscow. A lot of people thought that was going to affect the winter Olympics in Lake Placid. The next problem was the governor of New York, Hugh Carey, said on television, "Don't go to the winter Olympics in Lake Placid because the town's too small to hold the people and there won't be enough food there."

New York State built a prison in Saranac Lake, and before opening the prison, they used the buildings to house the Olympic athletes. By October, our sales were dismal, and we were running out of money. I caught wind of a travel show coming to Albany, New York, so I decided to rent a space to display pictures of Olympic events and hand out our brochures. I offered discounts for anybody who signed up at the show, but I came out of that show after three days without a single order. The next show we did was in New York City at the Javits Center. That show drew thousands of people. We were advertising the Olympics and our packages on the Don Imus radio station. In his advertisement, he said, "You don't want to ride on the bus up to Lake Placid with people throwing up on you! Stay with Arlo Tours, they're right in the middle of the Olympics."

Even with all the advertisements, we could not generate sales. It was starting to feel like we were in deep trouble. What else could possibly go wrong? Well, we found out that the Olympic Committee was going to continue to sell tickets right through the Olympics, and they were opening an office in Lake Placid. In early December, the campground's owner dropped dead of a heart attack after we just finished renovating. His family wanted the total rental payment of 40,000 dollars upfront, or they wouldn't let us open the campsite. I met with Vincent to discuss if we should pay the 40,000 dollars or just give up on everything. We had most of the trailers in place and the contracts with the bussing company completed. We even hired a septic company to pump out the trailers. The project's planning part was perfect, but the marketing part of the project was a disaster. It was obvious we knew nothing about marketing. We decided to scrape up 40,000 dollars and pay the rent. We still had a chance to make some sales. I went with the project to try to take care of slow times in the construction industry, and what I accomplished was putting a 35-year business in its death throes.

We started cutting expenses from wherever we could. The easiest place was to stop paying withholding taxes to the state and federal. We had no choice; we needed to survive as long as we could. I remember being in Lake Placid, walking the campsite at night all alone. I looked at what we had accomplished; the trailers were in place, the roads were there, it was quiet... serene. I was really disappointed. I felt like I had jeopardized the jobs of all the people who worked for me, not to mention my family and our home. I couldn't sleep that night. I had to fix it, but I had no idea how. One night, I was in the office in Peekskill about four weeks before the Olympics started. It was just me, Vincent and my cousin

Jo Bo. I told Vincent I was not going to stay in Peekskill and go broke.

He asked, "What can I possibly do about it?"

"I'm taking all the tickets and I'm going to Lake Placid where the action is."

The next day my cousin Jo Bo and I headed to Lake Placid. I had no idea what we were going to do, but we were going to do something.

CHAPTER XIV
It's Never Over Until It's Over

Meet Joe Bo, aka Joey, Joe, Bo, or anything in between. You should have met my cousin Joe Bo at the beginning. His mother and my mother were sisters. We grew up in the same town and did everything together as we grew older. He was a little younger than me, so he had some keeping up to do in the early years! Jo Bo was also working at Westchester Air Conditioning, Vincent's other business that we housed on Arlo Lane. Joe Bo and I rode into Lake Placid early in the afternoon. We stopped by Mike Nichols Pizza restaurant to get the local scoop. Mike knew the situation; he'd been involved with me from the beginning.

I went in to ask him if we could park our borrowed Winnebago behind his restaurant and put a sign in his window to advertise our Olympic tickets for sale. Of course, he said yes, so Joe Bo and I set up behind the restaurant. By late afternoon we had sold 2,500 dollars worth of tickets. That was the most action we had so far. At about ten o'clock that night, I told Joey we weren't going to make it selling tickets out of this Winnebago; we needed a storefront on Main Street. He laughed at me and said that everything in town had been rented five years ago, and there was no way we were going to find a storefront in the center of the Olympics. "Let me see you pull that one out of your butt!"

I left the Winnebago and took a walk up main street. It was about 10:30 at night. I walked the entire street on both sides. Everything was already taken. I kind of knew that. Then, I spotted the barbershop. I looked inside and noticed that the chairs were still in place and all the barber's products were still on the shelf. I immediately went back to Mike's Pizza and asked Mike if he knew the guy that owned the barbershop. He said,

"You mean… Norm's barber shop? Yeah, he's a good friend of mine."

"Give him a call, I need to talk to him."

"Joe, it is 11 o'clock at night."

"Call him, let us see if he is up."

He was up, and Mike gave me the phone.

"Hi Norm, I'm a friend of Mike's. Are you going to stay open during the Olympics?"

"Yes."

"How much money do you think you'll make cutting hair during the Olympics?"

"A couple of thousand dollars."

"Norm, I'll give you 6,000 dollars to rent me your store for the Olympics. You can take off and enjoy everything else that's going on."

"Okay, you have a deal."

"I need you to take out the barber chairs and remove the barber pole from the building."

He agreed, and just like that, we were back on track with a storefront! When I got back to the Winnebago, Jo Bo asked me where I was. I told him, "It takes a little bit of time to pull a storefront out of your butt."

The next day, Norm met me at the barbershop. I gave him the six thousand dollar check and hoped it didn't bounce. Norm took down the barber pole and took out the chairs. I called the shop in Peekskill to tell them I needed signs made for the store windows. When we woke up that morning, the Winnebago's heat was off because we had run out of propane. Perfect timing for Joe Bo and I to move into the barbershop for the duration of the Olympics. We slept on the floor and lived on pizza, beer, and cigarettes. It felt like we were teenagers again! Good thing the Olympics were only a few weeks long. That night, the signs were delivered, and by the next morning, we were up and running.

My friend and old army buddy, Ron Morrison, took a few weeks off from his job and came up to help me. He was a detective in Westchester County. By 10 o'clock that first morning, two hours into our new operation, we had zero sales. Twenty miles outside of Lake Placid, there was the parking lot where all the attendees had to park and bus in. I said to Ronnie, "Let's grab some tickets, drive to that parking lot and see if we can sell any." That's what we did. When we got down there, the cars were pouring in. I started trying to sell tickets to people coming into the parking lot. Again, no takers. I was totally bummed out.

We had left Joe Bo at the store. When we pulled into Lake Placid, there was a long line outside of my store! I couldn't believe my eyes. We parked the car and went into the store. Joe Bo was by himself, and he was overwhelmed. He was yelling at people to get in line. Ronnie and I jumped in and started selling. The tickets that we received from the Olympic committee had clipped corners. This meant that if you had a clipped ticket, you had to ride on my buses, not the Olympic buses. So any tickets that were sold at the shop needed to include bussing, parking, and housing. Therefore, we could sell clipped tickets above face value. A top skating ticket alone was 35 dollars, but I sold it for 350. We had some hot tickets and some not-so-hot tickets. We would be wheeling and dealing on everything.

The next day a reporter came in to talk to me. I told him the story about how much trouble we were in. The next day, the front-page headline of the Montréal News read, "If you need tickets for the Olympics, see Joe at the clip joint."

The next thing I knew, the phone was ringing off the hook! I called Norm and told him to put the barber pole back up so people would know how to find us. I had six phone numbers in Peekskill with people ready to answer, but The Montréal newspaper put the wrong phone number in the newspaper. I was pissed about that! They put the number for Norm's Barber Shop instead of my office number, and Norm's Barber Shop only had one phone line. I called the phone company, and I told them I needed four lines installed immediately at Norms Barber Shop. The operator told me I was using the phone illegally and she would shut the service off. I said to the operator, "Let me tell you a little story." I told her what was going on. Then I said to her, "Let's make believe I never called you." She said, "I can do that."

Ronnie's job was to answer the phone and give them the correct number to call for tickets. That's what he did all day long! After a few hours, I looked over, and Ronnie was leaning against the wall with the phone off the hook. I said,

"Ron, what the hell are you doing?"

He said, "I can't do this anymore."

"Yes, you can, now go back to work!"

My brother from California stopped in to see how I was doing. His company booked a complete package for sixty people from a different tour operator. Maybe he didn't know I was selling tickets? You think? There were reporters all over town looking for hot stories, so that's what I gave them. The story was picked up on national T.V. of me selling tickets in the barbershop. The more news stories that came out, the busier we were. My uncle called

and told me to get off the television and sell tickets. I said to him,
"What do you think is selling tickets?" Every day was more
interesting than the one before.

The Olympic Committee was selling tickets right next door.
They opened at 10 o'clock in the morning, so I opened at 7. They
closed at 8 p.m., so I closed at 11 p.m. They wouldn't take cash,
and I'd take whatever I could get. After a few days, we had the best
running operation in Lake Placid. We knew when the events were.
If we had tickets for that event that were unsold three hours before
the event, we then gave the tickets to a couple of kids we hired to
be our runners. We sent them to the event to sell them for whatever
they could get. We knew which tickets were hot and which were
not. Our buses ran on time, and the campsite ran well.

The Olympic Committee was selling tickets right next door,
but people preferred buying the tickets from us. Most of the time,
the Olympic Committee staff didn't know what they were doing in
that office. One night, we were getting ready to close at 11 o'clock
when six guys from Kentucky strolled into our shop. They were all
judges. They asked, "What events do you have for us to see
tomorrow?" They took out a jar of Moonshine, and we sat down
with them. We discussed what they could see while drinking. They
walked out with a lot of tickets that first night. They came back
every night for the next five nights. We made thousands from them
and drank a lot of Moonshine!

The town was alive, and in turn, we were alive. Most of our sales were cash, and we had piles of it. We were selling out about 40 percent of the trailer rentals on the weekend. They were selling packages in Peekskill with tickets I didn't have, so I had to go out on the street and buy tickets to fill their packages. Charlie Walsh, my attorney, closed his office for the Olympics to all his clients except for me. He would come in every day to see if I had any problems that we needed to work out.

The first event was the opening ceremony. We had managed to sell every ticket we had to that event. The next day, the newspaper had an article that said the only buses that were on time for that event were Arlo Tour buses. Every day reporters would come in, and I would tell them what they wanted to hear. I heard that one of the vendors complained to the Olympic Committee about them continuing to sell tickets after the August cutoff date. They agreed to exchange some tickets for the other vendor. I took my lawyer Charlie and a bunch of low-value tickets to the Olympic Committee's office and exchanged them for better class tickets.

One day, I looked up, and there was a man in a suit standing in front of me. He said, "I'm the Assistant Attorney General for New York State and I'm getting reports that you are scalping tickets here." There was a small window box in the front of the store. I said to him, "Sit down, let's talk." I told him the entire story about how we got screwed by the Olympic Committee and that I was not scalping tickets. I was charging the face value for the tickets and charging extra for bussing, parking, and housing, which I had to carry with my tickets. After a while, he said to me, "Keep doing what you're doing, we'll figure it out after the Olympics." *I'm either very lucky, or I'm very good at talking, I'll take either one.*

I was still taking care of the other two businesses while I was living on the barbershop floor. Elmsford Sheetmetal was bidding for a very large job for Nestlé's corporation in White Plains, New York. *It could be our ticket out of trouble,* I thought. My office sent the paperwork for that project up to the barbershop. I went over the paperwork and put a final price on it. The job was too big for most of the competitors in my area. They were coming from out of town for this job, so I needed to beat them.

Vincent went down to New York City to negotiate the job with a good customer of ours, Kirby Saunders. With a couple of days left for the Olympics, he called me and told me we got the Nestlé's job. It was great news. Now I needed to change my story to reporters about doom and gloom. I started telling them that it looked like we were going to make it after all. We needed to show that we were back in a position of strength. The paper printed a great article about us. The next day Vincent called to tell me that because of the article, Nestlé had taken the job from us. They did not want their name in the paper. What a disaster! I got on the phone with my contact from Kirby Saunders and talked about what we could do to get the job back. After a couple of conference calls, thankfully, we got the job back. There were only a few days left up there, and I had not been to an Olympic event yet. The USA vs. Russia hockey game was the hottest event of the year. I was selling the ticket for 550 dollars each. I saved four tickets for that game; myself, Joe Bo, Ronnie, and my Elmsford VP Don Trier took the night off to have some fun. Don had been handling all the activity at the trailer site and had done an excellent job.

That night, we saw one of the best hockey games ever. It was called "The Miracle On Ice." The U.S. A. team was never supposed to be able to beat Russia. The next night, Joe Bo and I were counting the money when Vincent walked in and said, "Just stick the money in the case, I will count it when I get back." I looked at Joe Bo, he looked at me, and I said, "No problem, Vincent, we got it. We are almost done counting." It was blood money I was counting and carrying it out of there… We spent too many nights on the barber shop's floor for me to let even one cent go unaccounted for. On the last night of the Olympics, Joe Bo, Ronnie, and I put the money into a suitcase. We counted 450,000 dollars and brought it with us to a bar for cocktails. Ronnie was a cop; he had his gun on his ankle. You could not pay me any amount of money to do it again, but I was not sorry I did it. I learned a lot about myself. I learned that I was a problem solver. When most people went left, I would go right. I learned that when someone said the word *no*, I would hear *go*. I could think on my feet, and I was not afraid to pull the trigger. I don't believe these skills are learned; I believe you're born with them, and you have to dig down deep to find them and hope that they pay off!

CHAPTER XV

Out Of The Woods And Into The Forest

I met with Vincent back in our shop in Peekskill. We needed to set
our priorities. We reanalyzed our cash position, and it wasn't
looking good. However, a lot better than if I didn't go to Lake
Placid, but we were still in trouble. Vincent said the 450,000
dollars in cash would not get us out of trouble. His idea was to go
to Binions Casino in Vegas and put it all on one roll of the dice! If
we doubled our money, he figured we would be in good shape, but
if we lost it, we would not be in much worse shape than we
currently were. I thought he was joking, but I was wrong! I told
him there was no way I just spent over a month sleeping on a
barber shop's floor and working my ass off for every penny to just
throw it away on one roll of the dice. The only place I was taking
the money was to the bank. That would prove to the bank that we
were good businessmen worth investing in.

We still had one hundred trailers on the campsite that we had to
move. There was a large burned-out building across the street from
our shop where we could put the trailers while we tried to sell
them. We needed to set up a payment schedule to withhold taxes
that we didn't pay to the state and federal government when we
were trying to stay afloat. We needed to get the new job at Nestlé's

underway so we could create a cash flow. We also needed to file a lawsuit against the Olympic Committee for fraud. We set up an appointment with the bank. Vincent and I were in the car on our way when I admitted that I thought we weren't going to make it. He asked me if I wanted to quit. I said no, but I didn't know how we were going to get out of it. He told me if I wasn't going to quit, then when we walked into that bank, not to ask for money. He said instead to tell them how much money we needed, and if they couldn't give it to us, we would forfeit our loan. We owed the bank more money than we had assets. When we walked into the office, the first thing the banker said to me was,

"Don't tell me you need more money."

"George, I need more money or we might default on the loan."

I rolled out my chart and told him we could have it paid off in a year. George laughed, and so did Vincent. Then Vincent said,

"Joe, you might as well let him have that 100,000 dollars you left as a guarantee."

George said it would help. I didn't see that one coming. Boy, was I naïve back then. George gave us more money, not enough to get us completely out of trouble but enough for me not to quit.

All of our credit cards were maxed out. We were hoping to collect some old receivables we had due. I bid on another job to Bo Nielsen from Denmark. He was coming to my office to discuss the job. I took him to lunch, and on the way to lunch, I needed gas in my car. As I pulled up to the gas pump, I asked Mr. Nielsen if he was having trouble with credit cards being declined for no reason, and luckily he said, "Yes, sometimes." I was hedging my bet in case the gas station denied my credit card. Sure enough, it was declined, so I paid in cash. We had settled on a number for the job of 79,000 dollars, but the job wasn't going to be ready for a couple of months. I suggested to Mr. Nielsen that maybe he wanted to prepay for the job because of how the monies were fluctuating back-and-forth between our countries. I held my breath... He thought about it, and to my surprise, he agreed that it made sense. That 79,000 dollars brought our company back to life!

The next problem we had was selling the 100 trailers as fast as we could. Every day those trailers sat was another day we were paying interest on the loan. As broke as we were, we hired a company to move all the trailers from Lake Placid to our shop. When all the trailers were back, we advertised an auction to sell them. We set the auction for a Saturday. By auction day, we had plenty of people waiting for a bargain. We paid 5,500 dollars per trailer. The auction started at 6,000. No bids. We dropped down to 5,500. No bids. 5,400, 3,500, and still no bids. I realized that nobody was going to bid on a trailer when there were 96 of them sitting there. I canceled the auction— time for plan B. The only problem was, I didn't have a plan B.

After a couple of days, I moved two trailers up to the upper parking lot and put an advertisement in the paper. The ad read two 24 foot, almost brand-new trailers used for the 1980 Winter Olympic for sale. Whenever someone showed up to look at the trailers and asked about all the other trailers that were sitting in the lot, I would tell them all the other trailers were already sold to a construction company in Saudi Arabia, and these were the only two we had left. That was how we sold every trailer for almost what we paid for them.

My shop Forman Frank Suda became a used trailer salesman along with running the shop. We unloaded 96 trailers in less than six months. I set up a meeting with the Federal and State Tax Department to come up with a payment program to pay back the money I owed them. The representative from the Federal Tax Department that I was assigned was very reasonable, and we worked out a payment plan. The representative from the State Tax Department was a real creep. He read me the Riot Act, threatening to put me in jail. He said to me,

"I see you have a partner, where is he?"

"He's in Florida for the winter."

"You mean to tell me he owes us this kind of money and he's in Florida?"

He went on for another 20 minutes or so and then agreed to give me a payment program. It looked like we were going to survive the fiasco of the Olympics. Big lesson learned; if you can't make money in the business you know, you have no chance to make money in any business you don't know. Stick to what you know.

CHAPTER XVI

Out Of The Ashes

The rest of 1980 seemed to be a good year. It looked like there was a lot of work on the horizon. We had already expanded the building. We had a new drafting department, and we upgraded the equipment in the shop. We hired a new estimator; he was 80 years old; *he should know the construction industry inside and out!* Our accountant had now been preparing the company-certified statements. With the statements, we would've been able to get the bonding to do larger jobs. My three part-time secretaries were working out well too. They couldn't read my writing, so I had to dictate the letters I wanted them to write. I had to make a change because they kept laughing at my spelling. I was still looking for a bookkeeper. The last good bookkeeper I had was Florence, Pete's sister. She quit when Pete did. Since then, we had gone through four others who had no idea what they were doing. My accountant recommended a woman for the position he had worked with for years at another construction company.

***

Meet Lorraine Edge. She came on board just after the Olympics when the company was in a weak financial position. Vendors were regularly calling for payments that we were not yet

149

prepared to give. She was a Godsend. Most of my competition had been coming from out-of-state. One of the big players was the McBride company in Northern New Jersey. They had been taking sheet metal work in my area for years. Their shop was larger than mine, so they were tough to compete with. It seemed like every time they took a large sheet metal job in my area; they lost money on the sheet metal portion of the job because of the union situation. Out of town contractors were only allowed to bring two of their union men onto the job site; the rest they had to hire from the Union Hall. These guys were not the cream of the crop. In my union local, I had the right to hire and fire. I'd been building my team now for the last seven years. I treated my men with respect, and they knew I used to be one of them. I had an open-door policy. If anyone had a problem, they could come directly to me. I had the strongest union team around, and it was time to kick this company up to the next level.

I got a call from the manager who was running the McBride's sheet metal shop. Meet Frank Candela, who was about my age. I found him to be very knowledgeable in the business. He said they just took a large job in my area, and he would've liked to start working with me on some projects. To start this relationship, he wanted me to fabricate the ductwork for the job he was starting. The McBride company was doing a volume of about 50 million a year. My company did not have the credentials to do a three or four-million-dollar sheet metal job. We had the ability, but not the credentials. We settled on the price for the fabrication job. I helped them pick out laborers for installation on the job. This was the start of a long relationship with the McBride company, their sheet metal company, Independent Sheet Metal, and Frank Candela.

***

By 1981, we were well underway on the installation of the sheet metal ductwork in the Nestlé's building. We still had a cash problem which was about to be fixed. In the middle of the Nestlé project, IBM decided to buy the building. Of course, we had to change almost everything we put in so far to fill IBM's needs. This change doubled the contract price and tripled our profit. During that year, we also had about four other jobs running. One of them was a General Motors job.

By 1982, we were in great financial shape. My accountants were producing good certified statements, which enabled us to increase our borrowing line at the bank. It was very important to us; it took a lot of money to start these larger jobs. I finally had the bookkeeper that would've helped us get to the next level. She knew construction accounting inside and out, and there was a very large IBM job coming up. Without a track record for doing these large jobs, we won't be invited to bid. I called my new friend Frank Candela at Independent Sheet Metal and asked him to meet up with Joe McBride, the president of McBride Mechanical. I knew that the McBrides were interested in bidding the job, and I wanted to see if they might be interested in a joint venture on the sheet metal portion. Joe McBride was a World War II fighter pilot. He was a real gentleman, and we got along great. We put the joint venture together, and we made a hell of a team. Frank Candela would take care of all the paperwork, and I would take care of the workers on the job site, which were all my workers. The job went very well. Towards the end of the job, IBM gave us a schedule of completion. After reviewing that schedule, I knew the schedule was impossible to complete. Not one trade could complete the job on that schedule.

Joe McBride and I went to a meeting on the job site in their trailer. The meeting started with the IBM executive asking each trade if they could complete the job as per their schedule. As it went down the line, every contractor confirmed they could do that. While they were talking, I folded my schedule into the shape of an airplane. When it came time for me to answer the question, I asked them if they could open the window. They asked,

"Why, are you hot?"

"No, I want to take this schedule and fly it right out the window. Not one of these contractors has any chance of bringing the job in on your schedule. They're just afraid to tell you. I am not going to spend hundreds of thousands of dollars to try and make a schedule that's not real."

I thought Mr. McBride would be mad at me; instead, he started laughing, and he agreed with me.

On another job, Joe McBride and I were at a pre-award meeting. Joe asked me in front of everybody if I was going to jump on the table and start kicking the paper off the tables like I usually did. I said to Joe, "Don't tell them that until after they give us the job."

One time, Mr. McBride called me up and said I double dipped him on extras on a job. I said, "Joe, I didn't double dip you ever." I went down to his office, and when I walked in, I had an ice cream cone for him with two scoops of ice cream on it. We had a great relationship and did a lot of work together. The joint ventures helped us build our reputation and confirmed that we could do any size job throughout our industry.

CHAPTER XVII

What Did You Do Now, Joseph?

The local union area we worked in was from the New York City line to Albany, New York, bordered by Connecticut. Outside of that area, we had to conform to the two-men union rule. For that reason, 98 percent of our work was in our local area. The productivity loss for installation outside of the area could be as high as 60 percent, and 80 percent of our contract price was labor. If you made a mistake on your labor, you could see big losses. That was why it was so important to stay in my local area and have my job costing correct before I started bidding for bigger jobs.

By the end of 1982, work was becoming scarce after the Jimmy Carter years in our area. The International Union started to merge small locals together. Our local number was 38, the Connecticut local next to us was local 39. They had less than half the men in their local than we did. The International Union decided to merge these two local unions, which would've greatly opened up the areas we could work in with our men. Stamford, Connecticut, was in this local area, and it had plenty of construction work there.

My uncle Vincent sat on the International National Labor Relations Board with the President of the International Union. His name was Ed Carlo Junior, the son of the Union President who retired. Vincent had his assurance that the Union merge was going ahead. Local Union 39 would be merged into Local Union 38. With the merge sure to happen, we decided to bid on two large jobs in the Connecticut Local 39 area. One was Pitney Bowes, and the other was First Stamford Place which had three office buildings. We believed that by the time we did the drafting and fabricated the duct, the merger would be complete, and we could use our men on the job site. We won both projects and started working on them. By the middle of 1983, we were ready to man both jobs.

The Union merge was yet to happen. We started Pitney Bowe's job with two of our men and two men supplied by Local 39; it was manageable. First, Stamford Place's job had three buildings. We broke these into three different jobs so we could put two of our own men on each job. This helped for a while, but we knew that when both jobs started rolling, we would have to hire more Local 39 men; that was when the problems started. The more men we hired, the less productivity we were getting. We were losing more money each day, but there was not much we could do about it. The merge was not going to happen for another year. We were pretty frustrated after all the hard work we had to do to get back on our feet after the Olympics. Do you know what the worst thing about almost going broke is? Doing it for a second time.

There was a large IBM job being bid on in our area. It consisted of three office buildings and a large central building. We were not involved in the original bids, but the job came over budget, and IBM rejected the bids. Joe McBride called me into a meeting and said IBM wanted the McBride company to look at the job to see if they could do a redesign and bring it back into budget. He gave me a set of drawings to take back to our shop to check what we could do with the sheet metal portion of the job to save money. The job was designed around low-pressure rectangular ductwork. I called the company that had a new system of high-pressure round spiral ductwork. With this system, we could reduce the sheet metal cost of the job by 40 percent. I made a detailed drawing of one section of the building, laid out with the new high-pressure spiral duct. Joe McBride set up a meeting with IBM and the engineer in New York City to present our changes. At that meeting, I presented my drawing with the new round spiral duct. The engineer stated that there was not enough room in the ceiling for the round duct, so they used rectangular ductwork instead. I had made another drawing showing a cross-section of the building with the round duct fitting in the ceiling. My friend Mayo Borman, who headed up the construction division of IBM, asked the engineer, "Will this system work?" After a little back and forth, the engineer said it would work. IBM gave us the job. Once a week, I would go to New York City and work on the design with the engineers and IBM. It became the largest job we had ever completed.

One day, I returned to the office after a meeting in New York City with IBM, and the office was in chaos. Vincent was there, and when I asked him what was going on, he said,

"I just came back from Pitney Bowes in Connecticut and I fired the foreman."

"You fired Billy?" I asked.

"Yes! I walked into his office and he had his feet up on the desk and the guys in the field were doing nothing."

"Vincent, Billy's not the problem, we are the problem. We should not have taken the jobs in Connecticut without the merger. We took a calculated risk that didn't work, it's not my guys' fault."

"I don't care, that's what I did and I'm sticking with it." Vincent yelled.

"Then you're sticking alone because I quit. You want to run this place? Then run it!" I said, and I walked out.

I spent the next couple of days looking around for an office to run East Coast Sheet Metal, my computer company out of. I called Vincent and told him that I would continue to go to the IBM Somers job meetings until the design was completed. About a week went by before I had a meeting with Vincent to see if we could resolve our problem. We agreed that he would come and talk to me about any problem with the manpower and that Billy would be hired back. We were near finished with both projects before the merge actually happened. In one of my trips to the job site before this, I told the guys from Connecticut who are working for me, "When the merge is complete, don't expect to work for me." And I never hired any of them.

When we bought our first house, it was on Lovell Street, in Lincolndale, NY. For almost a year, we had lived in that house before we realized that Lake Mahopac, the lake where Frank and I used to ski when we were teenagers, was less than a half a mile away! We would go to work every day in the opposite direction. What a surprise it was when we took a ride in the other direction. Ever since that day, I really wanted to have a house on the lake. I started looking for houses or properties around 1978. Every single available house on that lake was financially out of our reach. In 1981, my wife and I went looking at properties with the realtor. We found two pieces we liked. Both of them were around 55,000 dollars. Again, just out of our reach. They were both three-quarters of an acre and right on the lake. The realtor told me he had one other piece of lakefront property, but he didn't think we would like it. I said, "We are here, we might as well look at it." He showed us a piece of property on two and a half acres of land, right on the lake, with a waterfall running through it. As we pulled into the property on a dirt driveway, we couldn't see the lake because of the overgrowth. I found an old milk carton and stood on it so I could see a beautiful view of Lake Mahopac.

Barbara and I walked through the weeds towards the lake and saw the beautiful stone wall spillway and waterfall. The realtor told us the local synagogue donated the property, and they were really interested in selling it. We put an offer in at 35,000 dollars. They came back at 37,000 dollars, and we bought it. The First thing we needed to do was see how wet the property really was. I hired a consulting engineer. He told us we needed to put a foot drain all the way around the property to keep the road water from washing into the land. They also discovered there were springs four feet down, so we wouldn't have been able to build a home with a basement. We began to design a two-story, four-bedroom, 4,000 square foot house. A circular, two-story living room would be the focal point of the house. It would have a large fireplace and floor-to-ceiling windows overlooking the lake. The room would be three feet higher than the rest of the house to optimize the view. A balcony in front of the master and guest bedroom would overlook the circular living room giving the best lake view in the house. I did a design on paper and then built a scale model of the house to see how the round living room would fit into the roof.

When my wife and I were satisfied with the design, we hired an architect to complete the working drawings. We built the house in 1982. We put our existing house on the market and sold it pretty quickly. I gave the new buyer a date for when our new house would be complete. We didn't quite make that date, so we had to move into the new house without a few minor things. We had no kitchen for a few weeks, and only one of the three bathrooms was functional. Otherwise, it was perfect!

CHAPTER XVIII

Taking East Coast To The Next Level

By 1982, I had rewritten my labeling program onto the radio shack computer. We were starting to get a lot of interest in this product. I had hired my friend John Pauski as a salesman for the labeling system. I also approached my computer salesman Lonnie to come to work for me. We had a meeting set up to go over the details of the job. At the end of the meeting, Lonnie said he didn't think he could take the job. As he was walking out, I mentioned that the job came with a company credit card. He stopped, turned around, and took the job. We started aggressively marketing the labeling system, and one day I heard that a company developed a plasma cutting system to cut out the patterns for the sheet metal fittings. I told my salesmen that if this were true, nobody would buy a labeling system when they could buy a system that could cut out the fittings. It was the beginning of a long weekend, and I got a call at home from John. He said to me,

"Union Carbide called, you know the guys that make the batteries?"

"What did they want?" I asked.

"They noticed our labels on ductwork in one of their buildings and wanted to know if we could write a program to drive their plasma cutting system."

"What did you tell them?"

"I told them you would be back in the office on Tuesday."

"Call them back and tell him we'll be in *their* office on Tuesday."

That Tuesday, Lonnie, John, and I flew out to Indianapolis, Indiana, to the L-TEC division of Union Carbide. I told my guys if we could create this software for their plasma cutter, it would put us back in business. I was hoping we could get five thousand dollars for our software program. We sat in the conference room in front of a big blackboard. The head man for L-TEC was Fred Sassay. There were four other men in that meeting. They began by telling us a story of how they were working with the Lock Former Company to provide them with a plasma cutting machine for their computerized duct layout system. After they completed their work, Lock Former went with one of their competitor's machines... they were not happy campers. They wanted to produce a better and cheaper system than Lock Former. The price of the Lock Former plasma duct cutting system was 120,000 dollars. What they wanted to do was put their plasma cutting system on the market for 69,000 dollars. They started putting numbers on the blackboard. What would it cost on their end to put the system together, including marketing, sales, hardware, and profit?

As they put all their numbers on the blackboard, I added them up in my head and realized there were 15,000 dollars left over. That's when he asked me what my software was going to cost. I said 15,000 dollars. When they added my numbers to the bottom of their numbers and came up with the 69,000 dollars, they started slapping high fives with each other. We made the deal. When we left the meeting, I told Lonnie and John that we really stepped into it now. That was way over my head. I had no idea how to get it done!

When we got back to New York, we found an IBM personal computer for sale down in New Jersey. They had just come onto the market. I sent Lonnie down to pick it up and told him to find us a programmer.

* * *

Meet Jerry Seidman, a six-foot-two, 19-year-old computer nerd. His specialty was mathematics and computer software. He lived in New York City and did not have a driver's license. I picked him up at the train station and brought him to our office to talk about the project we were starting. I took him into the shop and showed him how we made fittings and labels. He said he could write the program, so I hired him on the spot. The next day, I set him up on the new IBM personal computer on a desk next to mine.

That morning, Vincent came in at about ten o'clock, and I introduced him to Jerry Seidman. Vincent sat down at his desk and started reading the paper. Jerry was sitting at his desk with his hands behind his head, looking at the computer screen. By quitting time, Jerry had not moved, and Vincent didn't look too happy. The next day, Vincent came in at ten o'clock, and Jerry was sitting at his desk with his hands in the same position as the previous day, behind his head. By two o'clock, Vincent called me into the hallway and said, "How much are you paying that guy? He hasn't moved his hand off the back of his head in two days." I said, "Vincent, he's working all the stuff out in his head. When he starts typing he's going to type fast."

In the meantime, L-Tec sent us a plasma cutting system that we had set up in the shop. They also sent a complete set of instruction manuals on their controller, which Jerry had to study and understand. Within a few days, Jerry had the plasma cutter moving under the control of the IBM personal computer.

We had about three months before the big show where we would introduce our new system. There was a lot of work to do in a very little amount of time. About two weeks after the initial plasma machine movement, we were ready to cut our first fitting. We were all standing around the plasma cutter, including Vincent. The machine came to life! The plasma torch fired up, and the machine cut our first fitting. That was the first time Vincent or anybody in the shop watched a machine layout and cut a sheet metal fitting. I never saw so many jaws drop in my life. We still had a tremendous amount of work to do, but it suddenly all seemed possible.

We worked every day, seven days a week. I was back to putting in 70 hours a week. One night when we were getting close to the show date at about 11 o'clock, Jerry said he couldn't work anymore. I said, "Lay down and take a nap for a few hours." He laid down and fell asleep right away. We let him sleep for two hours, and then we set all clocks ahead, so he thought he had a six-hour nap. He got up and went back to work. Jerry Seidman was one of the smartest guys I ever met.

L-TEC wanted to invite a few contractors to preview the software and the machine prior to the big show. The software wasn't ready, but it was good enough to demo. Lonnie and I flew back to Indianapolis to give a presentation to the contractors. The top guys wanted to see the presentation before we gave it to the contractors; I started showing them the software. They said to Lonnie,

"You can't have Joe give the demonstration, he doesn't know what he's doing."

"You don't understand, Joe. He didn't have any customers in front of him. He'll be just fine once there is a crowd," Lonnie responded.

That night, Lonnie and I went out for a few cocktails and got back late. The next day, I had about ten contractors in front of me. I started my presentation, and in minutes I had them nodding their heads "yes" in agreement with me. The reason I had them shaking their heads was because I was speaking their language. Engineers did not design my program. It was designed by a sheet metal contractor just like them. That's what separated our program from others. By the time we finished that demonstration, we had sold eight systems at 69,000 dollars each. When it was all over, the boss said to Lonnie,

"That was pretty smart of you guys, going back and working on that presentation last night."

"We didn't work on anything. We went out for cocktails all night long," Lonnie said.

The salesman from L-Tec said, "There's no way Joe ad libbed that presentation."

"That's what happens when you put customers in front of Joe," said Lonnie.

A few weeks later, we went to that show and sold 16 more systems off the floor. East Coast Sheet Metal was on its way.

While working with L-TEC on the plasma cutter, I was invited by them to the Indy 500 race. Their main headquarters was in Indianapolis, so they gave me six tickets to the race. I invited my Vice President Don Trier, my shop foreman Frank Suda, my two

East Coast salesmen Lonnie Brinker and John Pulaski, and my cousin Joe Bo. Six of us took our seats in the front of the aircraft. We had never seen seats like those before. Instead of being three seats across in a row, three seats were facing another three seats with a table in between; it was like we were sitting at a poker table! After takeoff, we ordered a round of Scotch and started playing cards. The next thing we knew, the stewardess brought us fresh-popped popcorn. By the time we landed in Buffalo, we had drunk all the Scotch on board. We stayed on the same plane for the next leg of the trip. They replenished their supply of Scotch for us, which we finished by the time we landed in Indianapolis.

We were feeling no pain when we went to pick up our Rent-A-Car. We had rented a station wagon that way; we could all fit in one car. We walked outside the airport, and there was a station wagon sitting there; it was already running. We threw our luggage in the back of the car and drove to our hotel. The night before the race, the President of L-TEC was having a get together at his house. Lonnie, John and I were going to go to the party. The other three guys were left back at the hotel since they were not directly involved with the business partnership.

When we got to the party, there was a reception line greeting everyone. Lonnie walked in first; he shook hands with Mrs. Tickjohn and then with Mr. Tickjohn, the manager of L-teck. They had a big Irish Setter sitting next to them, and Lonnie patted the dog on the head as he moved through the line. Next, John did the same thing. I walked through the line last. As I shook hands with Mr. TickJohn, the Irish Setter got up and stuck his face right into my crotch. Mr. Tickjohn apologized for his dog's behavior. The only thing I could think to say to him was, "How much do you want for this dog?" Everybody started laughing, and for the rest of the night, I hid from the dog.

The next day, the six of us went to the race. I thought it might be a little boring to watch cars go round and round the same track two times, but when they said, "Start your engines," and those cars came alive, it was very thrilling. We had great seats on turn number one, and we very much enjoyed that race. It was a trip to remember. When we got back to the airport at the end of the trip, I went up to the desk and handed them the keys and the contract for our rental car. They looked at the contract and said, "We are very sorry but according to our paperwork, you never picked up your rental car." We left the station wagon outside the car rental area and flew home. Apparently, we stole somebody's car for a week! It turned out that with the extra 450,000 people in Indianapolis, nobody noticed that we borrowed their car!

CHAPTER XIX
Ronald Reagan Era 81-89

By the beginning of 1984, the Reagan policy started to kick in. There were a lot of construction jobs in our area on the horizon. Elmsford Sheet Metal positioned itself to take full advantage of the boom in our area. The merge of Local 38 and 39 was finally complete, allowing us to use our own union guys on jobs in Connecticut. We landed four major jobs in a few months. A General Foods job in White Plains and three IBM jobs. Two of the IBM jobs were joint ventures with Independent Sheet-Metal. With these larger jobs, we were bidding against large out-of-town contractors. To be more competitive, I came up with a new policy to study these jobs during the bidding process and offer the buildings' owners valued engineering to save money. In the sheet metal industry, there are a lot of different ways to make the same ductwork. Some of my values were based on duct construction details.

To be efficient in the shop, we needed the duct construction details to match the machinery we had in place. Valued engineering became a normal way for us to bid on these large projects and still remain on budget. On one project, I gave a list of several value engineering items. New bid documents came out for the project,

and I noticed all my valued engineers were part of the bid. This
meant that all of my competitors could see exactly how we had
priced the job. It was information for the job owner alone, not for
the industry. I was not a happy camper about it, and I told the
contractors that they would be getting a total lump number for
value engineering on any further bids. They would only get my
breakdown after I won the job.

By 1986, we were underway with the IBM Somers job. It was a
very prestigious set of buildings designed by the famous architect
I.M. Pei. I would attend all of the following scheduling meetings
for these jobs. On this particular job, it was so prestigious that I.M.
Pei, second in command, was running the job for him. After every
meeting with all the contractors about the job scheduling, he would
call me into his office, shut the door and ask me, "Joe! What's the
real schedule, and what do we need to get this back on track?"
They knew that I always gave the true information. I told him what
I needed in order to get my work in on time, and he worked on
getting it done. One day, I was in their office in New York City,
and he brought me in to meet I.M.Pei. That was an honor! It was
the first famous architect I had ever met.

On top of all this work, we picked up two large General Motors
jobs in their Tarrytown plant. The plant was switching over to build
the new minivans. They required a completely new paint shop. The
job consisted of seven 400 foot-long spray booths and seven 400

foot-long ovens. It also included a large stainless steel cleanroom. We took the installation portion of the job from a company in Detroit named Try-Mark. They would supply all the material for the spray booth and the ovens. They did not ask me to bid on the installation of the cleanroom. I asked them, "Why not?" They told me they thought we had too much work and couldn't handle the installation. I told them I was not interested in the project without the cleanroom. Of course, I was bluffing, but it worked. We ended up with the cleanroom.

By 1986, we were running on all cylinders. We had added a new addition to the shop, updated our shop equipment, and added computer-assisted drafting that my software company developed. We were working in the shop on two shifts and six days a week. We enhanced our reputation by bringing all our projects in on time with quality work. Our workforce was the cream of the crop, and our turnover rate was still zero. If you needed a job done on time and correctly, the word on the street was to call Elmsford Sheet Metal. My prices were hard to beat on most jobs; *if I'm higher than my competition, they call me, and they give me what they call a "last look."* At which point do I go back to value engineering to try to get my price down? Sometimes I would tell the customer, "Fast, good or cheap; pick any two."

One time, I was called in to take a job at one of my competitor's prices. It was a large job, and I told them that the company you received the price from was not qualified. I had been working with a guy for a while, and he said to me, "Joe, you have to take the job at that price, otherwise they are going to make me give it to this guy." I told him to give the other guy the job, and when they would fail, I would come and pick up the job and make more money. He didn't like that answer, so he kept pushing me. Finally, I told him, "If I take this job, I'm going to have to screw you to make a profit." He laughed, and I took the job.

While doing the job every couple of weeks, I would go to his office to have him sign extra work orders. I went to see him one day, and he said to me, "You're screwing me with all these extra work orders." I sat across the desk from him, looking at the paperwork for this very large extra that my 80-year-old estimator gave me. I was trying to collect while he was complaining about the cost of the extra. There was a line on the paperwork where the estimate number should go. My estimator had written "64 Little Mother F…" He looked at it and said, "What the hell are little Mother F…?" I said, "I'm not sure, but knowing my estimator they're going to be very expensive. I told you I was going to have to screw you to make a profit. If I don't get them signed, I could lose my job." I said that a lot to him.

One day, we were walking across the roof, and he said to me, "Hey Joe, I have a large job in London I'd love you to run for us."

"I can't take the job before you even tell me how much you'll give me," I replied.

"Why is that?"

"Because I own half of this company."

"You've been telling me all this time that you would lose your job if I don't sign these extra work orders and you're actually a partner?"

"I had to make a profit!" I said.

Whenever they would come into my area, I would get the last look at whatever job they did.

In 1987, we landed another General Motors job. We hired a crane for the first part of the job to lift the air conditioning units up to the roof. There were 12 men scheduled on a Saturday to do the job. That morning I got a call from my general foreman telling me that the ironworkers were claiming that it was their work and they would not let the crane hookup. "I will be right down," I said. My guys were standing around, and the ironworkers were standing around too. It was a very tense situation; the last thing I wanted to see was a fight on the job. There was a big ironworker standing on top of the track of the crane. I said to my foreman, "I'm going to go up to talk to him. If anybody starts a fight, they're fired and if he hits me, catch me."

I jumped up on the crane, and I took out my union book. I said to the big ironworker,

"Right here in this book it shows that this is our work."

"I can't read," he responded.

That was it; we were at a stalemate. The ironworkers had tied the crane to the steel of the building so it couldn't move. We backed off the job that day, and we filed an emergency claim with the courts for labor relations. Within a week, we had a court date. I told Vincent I was too busy to take care of this; he had to go to that court hearing. He argued that I knew more about the case than he did, but he agreed to go. Of course, he added,

"Wait till you see the lawyer that's taken this case for us. This woman has the largest boobs I've ever seen and she is beautiful."

"Oh okay, I'll go do the court thing."

I was on the witness stand talking to the judge, and I said that the ironworkers tied the crane's hook to the building steel. The judge asked them if that was correct. The ironworkers answered,

"We only did it for a little while."

We won the case. When I got back to the shop and walked into the office, Vincent started laughing. He asked,

"Well… Did we win the case?"

"Yes, we won the case, and that trick about the pretty lawyer was not funny!"

Another interesting job was in 1989. It was at the Mamaroneck sewage treatment plant, and it was a large job with an interesting type of work. The plant was on the Long Island Sound; they had an

existing smokestack with a lighthouse on top that went back to the
1930s. We needed to put another liner in the smokestack without
disturbing the stack itself. We accomplished this by building it
from the bottom and connecting it one piece at a time. Then, we
lifted it from the top of the stack with chain falls. It also had a large
exhaust duct in the system, big enough to drive a car through. They
specified the ductwork to be built out of two-inch-thick reinforced
fiberglass. It was fireproof, with the ability to withstand a list of
chemicals they would supply to us. The duct's purchase cost was
over one million dollars, and the installation cost was three times
higher than a normal piece of duct. I offered them a voluntary
alternative to use 3/16 thick stainless steel instead of fiberglass,
and I would give them a 350,000 dollar discount. They did not
accept the voluntary alternate.

We went ahead, built, and installed the duct as they specified.
Towards the end of the job, they accidentally turned the wrong
valves and flooded the fiberglass duct with water. I got a call in the
office that we had a problem with our fiberglass ductwork. It was
delaminating, and we had to replace it. They wanted to meet with
me immediately. Before the meeting, I did a thorough check of the
specifications on the piece of duct. I copied the page of the
specification dealing with the duct and went to the meeting. There
were quite a few people in the meeting. The engineer said to me,

"Your duct is falling apart, you need to replace it at your own cost."

"Your guys flooded it with water," I said.

"It was supposed to be able to take the whole list of chemicals."

"I had the list of chemicals they supplied in their specification and water was not on it."

"You're not going there, are you?"

"Yes, I am," I continued, and I walked out of the meeting.

We went to several meetings back and forth on this problem. In one of the meetings, I walked in with duct tape on my jacket pockets. The engineer asked what the tape was for. I said, "Just to keep your hands out of my pockets." We agreed to coat the inside of the duct with a thin layer of a special product. We would split the cost three ways: 1/3 owner, 1/3 manufacturer, and 1/3 by me. This kept us out of court. At the end of the project, they had an awards ceremony. I was standing next to the engineer when they called me up and gave us a performance award. I came back and stood next to the engineer. I looked at him and said, "You didn't get one of these, did you?" We both laughed. Whenever he had a job in my area and had questions, he would call me.

***

Speaking of court cases, let's go back to that time in Lake Placid. Eight years ago, we filed a lawsuit against the Olympic

Committee for fraud, and the lawsuit was finally coming to court. I hired my local lawyer, Alan Singer, who had been with me for years. He and my Lake Placid local lawyer, Charles Walsh, were going to work together on it. The case was held up in Elizabethtown, NY, which was in the Adirondack Mountains. Alan would be handling the case in the courtroom.

For the first part of the morning, we were to pick a six-person jury. It started out pretty rough. When I was on the stand, Alan started asking me questions that I had no answers for. I had no idea which direction he was headed. Luckily, at lunchtime, I had a chance to ask him why he was asking me so many stupid questions. I told him, "You know what this case is about, start asking me the right questions, then I'll give you the answers." We went back to the courtroom. I was back on the witness stand, and Alan started asking me the right questions. The other lawyer was a young guy, and it seemed as though he built his case around the idea that I was a liar. He yelled, "Objection!" to all of Alan's questions. They emptied the courtroom and went to the backroom to discuss an objection. They left me in the courtroom by myself. I wandered around drinking water from the "other lawyers' pitcher," and sometimes maybe looking at his notes. This went on back-and-forth much of the afternoon.

The second day started pretty much the same way, except this time, he cross-examined me on the stand. He took out a copy of our brochure. On the cover of the brochure was a picture of the trailer we used during the Olympics. He says to me,

"Mr. Massaro, what size trailers did you use during the Olympics?"

"24 foot."

"Is this brochure completely accurate?"

"Yes, it is."

He pointed to the picture on the brochure and asked,

"Is that a picture of the trailer that you used during the Olympics?"

"Yes, it is."

"Mr. Massaro, that's not true. The picture on your brochure of the trailer is a picture of a 30-foot trailer, not a 24-foot trailer."

"Yes, that's correct."

"Then your brochures are not accurate like you said they were, you lied."

"The 30 foot trailer and the 24 foot trailer are exactly the same on the inside. The trailer manufacturer did not have a picture of the 24 foot trailer. But, if you look at the brochure, you will notice that the back end of the trailer is not shown in that picture. Only 24 feet of that trailer is shown."

He did not know what to say. I noticed a couple of the jurors were nodding in agreement. He went back to his podium to pour himself a glass of water, but there was no water left in his pitcher, only ice, which spilled all over the floor. I don't know how that happened!

By day three, we were in pretty good shape. Several other vendors testified that the Olympic Committee told them they would not be selling tickets after August. This trial was nothing but fun for me. I had already absorbed all my losses, and my companies were in excellent shape. The trial was more for my ego than anything else. When we got back from lunch on day three, the other lawyer was writing numbers on the blackboard... a lot of numbers. He turned the blackboard towards me and asked,

"Mr. Massaro, are these numbers correct?"

I looked at the blackboard and said, "No, they're not."

"Why are they not correct?"

"You added eight and five together and came up to 14. I did not go to college, but I know eight and five equals 13."

The jury broke out laughing, and the judge pointed towards me and said, "He's correct." He moved the blackboard back over to his desk, took out his adding machine, and started adding up all the numbers again. It took him another 15 to 20 minutes. He then turned the blackboard back towards me and said,

"Are they correct now?"

I said, "No, they're not."

Everybody looked at the blackboard. He said, "Why not now?"

"They are your numbers, not my numbers. Now let me give you the correct numbers."

The next thing he did was hand me my brochure again and asked me to explain it. My lawyer Charlie turned to my lawyer Alan and said, "Watch this." I spent the next 25 minutes going through every aspect of my brochure. My bussing, my parking, and my clip tickets. When we left the courtroom, Charlie said to me, "When you finished explaining that brochure, I wanted to buy tickets."

On day four, when we got into the courtroom, the judge called me into his chambers with my lawyers. He told me, "Mr. Massaro, you are kicking this guy's butt. But if you win this case, I can't give you any money. Settle the case."

"Why can't you give me any money?"

"Because they didn't break the law. You have to settle his case, or you'll get nothing. It was obvious that they screwed you, but they didn't break any laws. How much do you want to settle for?"

"Let them come up with a number."

We had sued them for 800,000 dollars. Even if we could get the money from the courts, the Olympic Committee had no money left. We settled at 75,000 dollars, and they had to pay me overtime from the collections they received from the ski jump. When the jury found out that we settled, the foreman came up to me and told me they were going to give me every penny. I thanked them. Another lesson learned! Vince always said, "If you have not made a bad deal, you have not made enough deals." Now it was time to go back to work.

CHAPTER XX
Changing Our Business Model

We had been subcontractors up to this point in our business. What that meant was, the owner of a new building hires a construction manager, the construction manager hires; an architect, structural engineer, general contractor, electrical contractor, plumbing contractor, and a mechanical contractor. We were subs to the mechanical contractor. Once a mechanical contractor was awarded a job, he would go out for a bid to find the lowest sheet metal price available. I wanted to eliminate the middleman and enable us to bid directly to the construction manager. This had not been done in our area yet. In order to accomplish this, several things had to be in place. We needed a track record for completing large projects, we needed to secure large performance bonds, and we needed a much larger line of credit at the bank.

I want to explain to you why this was such a big deal for our company. The mechanical contractor gets the job. In his bid, he puts pricing for the sheet metal ductwork, air handlers, air outlets, insulation on the duct, fans, air balancing, etc. Let's say I gave him a price to do just the sheet metal work for three million dollars. If he gets the job, he goes back to all the sheet metal contractors and tries to get a lower number. Now, he can probably buy the job from one of these contractors for two and a half million dollars. He just made an additional half-million dollars on this project! Besides that, he gets to buy the fans, air outlets, air balancing, and insulation.

On each one of these, he makes additional profits. If I get the job as a subcontractor, 80 percent of my cost is labor, and I have to wait for the mechanical contractor to get paid before I get paid. Most of the time, they cut my payment to give themselves a better cash flow. If I make a mistake on the labor, I'm screwed. If he makes a mistake on his labor, he can get additional money from his buyouts. The change would be huge for my company. It would increase our volume by 50 percent and give us better cash flow. This meant that we had to be very careful. We had to be completely ready, and once we made the move, we would likely make enemies out of the mechanical contractors that were currently giving us work. It is what they call risk and reward.

I began positioning the company to be ready for the move, but it would've taken years to get everything in place. I hired a new field coordinator, Heinz Meyer, and promoted several foremen up to general foremen. I also had a secretary, Robin Omara, who would be a great fit as the field super, so I shifted her position. We would have to spend some time adjusting our financials to be able to prove ourselves in the new position. Before we could bid on any job, this part would take a while to establish.

***

In 1989, we won a big job at Letterle Laboratories. The mechanical contractor was McBride, and the construction manager was Torcon. We knew there was going to be a lot more work coming out of this project. I needed to show Torcon what we could do. The sheet metal was the biggest part of the job. The construction manager called me into a meeting and said to me, "Joe, I want your company to be the pushers on this job. I need you to set the pace," and that's what we did. This could've been the first construction manager I approached to ask for a direct contract for the "air" side of the next job when we were ready.

CHAPTER XXI

Beating The Odds

By the end of 1990, our company was in the best shape of its life. My uncle Vincent wanted to get out while we were on top. He told me what he wanted: for me to buy out his 51% of the company, and that's what I gave him. I was now the sole owner of Elmsford Sheet Metal and East Coast Sheet Metal Fabricating Corp. I had been running both companies for the last six years basically on my own, with Vincent in more of a consultant role, so I was confident. I was thankful for the opportunity he gave me, and I was ready for my new direction.

It had been a long and winding road for me to get there; many things happened along the way. I lost my best friend: my father, early in my journey. He was with me when I became vice president and partner in the business in 1973. I lost him soon after that. I remember the words he said to my mother after one of my many failing report cards, "Don't worry about Joe, he'll do just fine." I probably shocked a lot of people, including myself. With the solid foundation and a fantastic team that I built, I was excited to see where I could take this.

I'd learned my lesson about taking jobs out of my local union area, or at least I thought I had, but some people just needed to learn the same lesson a few times before they would stick! In 1991, Frank Candela called me to tell me they had an opportunity to do a very large job at the General Motors plant in New Jersey. He knew I had experience with that type of work from doing General Motors jobs in my local area. He wanted to know if I would be interested in a joint venture project with him. This would be a little different because New Jersey was his local area. He would utilize his own men on this project. We could also supply more men than usual due to his contacts with the union. Frank and I met at his office to go over the project. The biggest problem with the job was the amount of time we would have to complete it. Christmas was right in the middle of the schedule. The key to success on this type of job was getting the planning done. Every hour had to be planned out. A lot of these jobs had penalties if you missed their completion dates. To bring the job in on time, we needed to work two shifts right through the Christmas holiday. We needed 30 men on each shift. Finding these men was not a problem because of how much money they would make. The job was loaded with overtime, and on the two days of Christmas, their pay would be four times more than usual.

We were pretty much on schedule coming into the Christmas week. We debated whether we should work Christmas Eve and Christmas Day. We decided we could not risk the chance to miss a deadline, so we had to work on both days. Try explaining that to your wife and teenage daughters. During the first shift on Christmas Day, we catered hot turkey dinners to be delivered to the plant. Frank Candela went to the job site on Christmas Day and had dinner with the men. I took the night shift; again, the turkey dinners were delivered to the job site, and I had dinner with the men that night. It was very important to the workers on the job site; they really appreciated it, and I enjoyed doing it. I remembered what it was like to be one of them. It felt good to be appreciated. The job turned out to be one of our best. I learned that the best way to be successful when taking work out of our Union area was to joint venture with a contractor in that area instead of trying to do it myself.

***

In 1991, I got another large job in the Ford manufacturing plant that was coming out in New Jersey. This job was bigger than the General Motors job we had just completed, and the completion times were worse. Frank and I were going to joint venture on this project too. We spent a couple of weeks on the bidding process. The scheduling was nearly impossible. To have any chance of completing the project on time, we could not be delayed by one day. It could've taken upwards of 200 men; that is a huge crew. We had to figure in all sorts of overtime.

We were called into a pre-award meeting at the Ford plant. They asked us if we could complete the project on time. I told them it would've been very tight. If we were held up at any place, even for a week, the cost overruns could've been in the seven figures. They gave us the job, and we started gearing up to go to work. Before we even got started, we were delayed for two weeks because they found asbestos in our area, and it had to be removed before we could begin our work; it immediately put us at a disadvantage.

We completed the job on time and put together a cost for the delay. It came to over one million dollars. We submitted the claim; then, the fun began. They thought we were crazy with our number and would not even discuss it. We turned the problem over to Frank's lawyer. The first meeting with Frank's lawyer, who I had never met, didn't go so well. He asked how much I was willing to settle for. I said to him,

"I'm not telling you that. I don't care if you're my lawyer, I know you'll just take that number and discount it."

"What do you want me to do?"

"Go with the total number that we submitted, it's the right number."

We had several meetings with Ford, but they did not go as planned. Our lawyer filed a lawsuit. Ford wanted to meet one more time before we went to court. We were sitting in Ford's conference room for about thirty minutes. The door opened, and Ford's in-house lawyer walked in. He was an older gentleman, so old I

thought to myself, *he must have worked for the original Mr. Ford.*
He said,

"I'm not giving your contractors ten cents!"

I said to the lawyer, "We told you in the pre-award meeting, if
we were delayed this is what would happen."

"You're going to have to prove that in court."

"That'll be easy enough."

"What do you mean?"

"You have the tape for that meeting, you can listen to it
yourself. The tape I have here proves the contractors knew about
this asbestos problem before awarding the job."

The lawyer then said to the Ford people, "You taped that
meeting?" When they answered "yes," the lawyer walked out of
the room, and we ended up getting paid for our claim.

With Vince's retirement, it was my turn to start getting involved
with the sheet metal contractors and the Union. We were the largest
contractors in our area, and it was important for us to have a good
relationship with the International Union, the local Union, and the
Contractors Association. My first position was to be the
Negotiating Committee chairman with the local union contract
coming up that year. I had a good rapport with the president of the
local union Charlie Hertell; we had lunch together before
negotiations started.

We set the parameters for our negotiations. The committee was made up of five contractors and five union leaders. Without the parameters set up, it would've been impossible for us to negotiate a contract. Both Charlie and I knew what we needed, and we negotiated to that point. I became president of the Local Association, Chairman of the Local Labor Management, and the Grievance Committee. I was also appointed to the National Labor Relations Board. The board resolved conflicts between labor and management throughout the United States.

At my first meeting with the board, I sat at a table with six people on the labor side, including the International Union president and six contractors on the other side. All I did was listen to get a feeling for what was going on. There was a problem between a local contractor and the Union. We discussed the problem at length, and we went out in the hall with the contractors to discuss what we should do. During the conversation, the contractor said that the Union was correct in this dispute, but we couldn't agree with them because we represented the contractors. I didn't say much. When we went back into the room, I sat on the side with the Union. My president said to me,

"Mr. Massaro, you're on the wrong side of the table."

My reply was, "Not on this issue."

I thought that might be the end of my four-year term! I sat on that committee for 12 years. I did not care what side you were on, but I cared about what was right. I had an advantage. I knew both sides well. When a tough dispute occurred, they sent me in with my counterpart from the Union side, who was the president of the Boston Local. His name was Joe Nigro; we became friends. I was from New York, so I was a pretty fast talker. Joe Nigro from Boston was a faster talker. At one of our meetings, the North Carolina contractors were having a dispute with their local union. They sent Joe and me into a meeting with them to try to resolve their problems. Joe and I started going back and forth in front of the group, arguing on each side. They settled the case quickly, and we headed into the big meeting to tell them that we settled. The president of the Union congratulated them on their settlement. One of the men from North Carolina said, "We had no choice but to settle; they both talked so fast we did not understand what them boys were talking about." Everybody in the meeting started laughing. When they had a tough problem in an area, they would send Joe and I in to try and resolve the issue, and in most cases, we would get it settled. Joe Nigro became president of the International Union. It's good to have friends in high places.

***

In 1991 I got a call from a sheet metal contractor in Kuwait. It was right after the war. He said he saw me at a show and wanted to know if I could come out there to help them modernize their sheet metal business. I said I would. Everybody in my shop thought I was crazy for going to Kuwait. They said the war just ended, and there was no food or water. I thought it would be interesting, so I went.

When I landed at Kuwait's airport, it was a zoo. Hundreds of people were crowding the information counter. I just sat back and analyzed what was going on. The next thing I knew, my name was being called out over the intercom. I found a man holding up a plaque with my name on it. I told him who I was and that I needed to get my luggage, but he already had it for me. I thought maybe this was not going to be so bad. We went out to his car and started driving to the hotel where I was to stay. Some areas still had smoke rising from the war. There was damage everywhere. *Maybe this wasn't a great idea.* When we got to the hotel, the man that picked me up said, "I will be here at 8 o'clock tomorrow morning to pick you up, do not get into anybody's car but mine." When I walked into the hotel, I noticed bullet holes in some of the windows. Inside, they had a buffet set up for lunch that ran from one end of the room to the other. That story about no food and no water was incorrect; it looked like all the food in Kuwait was on that table!

The next day at 8 am, the car was waiting for me outside. On the way to the office, I could see the devastation that happened in town. There were very large cement trucks sitting on blocks with their tires missing, impossible not to notice. When the Iraqi troops occupied Kuwait, they pillaged everything. When I arrived at the office, I met with the manager. We sat in his office drinking sweet tea, talking about what they wanted to accomplish. They had a new building they wanted to use for their shop. I walked through the building and took measurements of it. In the afternoon, I met with the number two son. Apparently, I had to get through the manager before I could talk to the son. When I started talking with the number two son, he told me what they wanted to accomplish. He saw my equipment at a show and wanted to buy it to modernize his shop. He mentioned that in his shop, his men could cut one sheet of steel a day. I told him with the equipment we could provide; he could cut 50 sheets per man per day. The next day, I again met with son number two. It was the same routine. They picked me up in front of the hotel and took me to their shop, but first, we drove into the desert to see the oil fires burning. It was just amazing. Then, he took me to his ocean view home. He showed me where they took all the electrical outlets off the wall. All the stuff they were stealing, they were sending back to Iraq.

On day three, I was outside at 8 o'clock in the morning. It was just as hot at 8 o'clock in the morning as it was at noon. A car pulled up; I thought the man said Joe, so I raised my hand and got into his car. We drove around the city for a while, and it was not the same as the days before. I ended up at some guy's office. He said to me, "I don't think you belong here." I happened to have a business card from the other company which I gave him. He called

the company, and they came to pick me up. When I got in the car,
the driver I used to be with said, "I told you not to get in anybody
else's car. It is very dangerous here." That day I negotiated a
contract with them for upgrading their shop. I would pick out all
the equipment they needed to buy, handle the purchasing and the
shipping of the equipment to them, create a complete layout of
their building to show where each piece of equipment would go,
provide qualified men to come to their shop, and train them on the
new equipment. For the service, I wanted 15% of their profits
above what they were making today for a three-year period. They
agreed, and we signed a contract.

At the end of the day, son number two told me,

"Tonight you will meet our father."

"Are you going to be there too?"

"No, you'll meet my father by yourself."

Before he drove me back to the hotel, he took me out to what
they called "The Road Of Death." It was the road leading back to
Iraq. Before the war ended, Iraq had a convoy heading back to
their country. The U.S. Air Force blew the convoy to pieces; there
were still bodies in the vehicles. To this day, Kuwait is a very
religious country; no alcohol, no women, and no improper
dressing. *I could be in big trouble here.*

That night at 6 o'clock, the car was waiting for me outside the
hotel. They took me to the father's 10,000 ft. bachelor pad in the

center of Kuwait. When I walked in, there were four older gentlemen there. One of them came up to me. He was dressed in traditional Kuwaiti attire and introduced himself as the owner of the company, the father. He told me to have a seat, then walked over to a cabinet and pulled out a bottle of Scotch. He sat next to me and said, "My sons are very religious, I am not." He turned on his big screen TV that had girls dancing on screen and said to me, "If it wasn't for the war, I would have had real girls dancing here." He was one of the richest men in Kuwait. I had a lot of fun that night, and at the end of the evening, he personally drove me back to the hotel. When I got back to New York, I put a complete package together with all the equipment he needed to buy, brochures of all the equipment, and a layout of the shop, which showed the equipment's exact placement. After a week or so, I called to see how they were doing and when they wanted to place the order. I found out they had already placed an order with a Japanese outfit. That was the last I heard from them. You can't win them all.

I had been doing a lot of IBM work over the years, and I still had a lot of contacts with them. The man who I met years ago, Mayo Borneman, was still in charge of the construction division. They had big projects coming into the Fishkill area. I was doing a large project for a mechanical company called Merrick Meridian. They had not paid me in months, and I was starting to get a little worried. They owed me 450,000 dollars. Normally, I would put a lean on the job, but I was delaying in doing it because of the IBM job. I got a call from my friend Mayo. He told me it looked like Merritt Meridian was going out of business and that I should put a lien on the job for the money they owed me. I took his advice and put the lien on the job.

I called Mayo to thank him for the heads up on the Merritt Meridian situation, and I asked him if we could set up a meeting to pitch my idea of splitting up a contract into what they call a "wet bid" and an "air bid". He liked the idea; he wanted us to sit down with the construction manager, who happened to be Whiting Turner. I had done a lot of work with that construction manager, and we had a good relationship with them. We set this meeting up to go over just how the bid would be broken up, like what would be in the air contract and what would be in the mechanical contract. We would have no overlaps or missing items. One of the questions they had was, "Can you put up a performance bond?" And my answer was "Yes." We ended up bidding all the IBM work in Fishkill as a prime contractor on the Airside.

I already had an office in Fishkill with the team doing all of the IBM maintenance work. The office was run by one of my men. They called him "Joe Pretty"; he had been around for a while, and IBM liked him. Merit Meridian ended up going out of business. IBM called me and suggested that since I already had an office in

Fishkill, I should take over the piping maintenance for them. All of Merit Meridian's workers were available. I said I needed to think about it and would get back to them soon. I went up to meet Joe Pretty and asked him what he thought about the idea and if he could run it.

"Yes, I can!"

I said to Joe, "I know nothing about piping, so my rule is very simple. Bring me a profit or I shut it down."

He agreed, and West Tech International was formed. We worked out of a barn in Fishkill, New York. The work we were doing required cleaning piping for their chip manufacturing. In the barn, we built a 10.000 particle class cleanroom— the only one in the area. West Tech grew so much over the next two years that we ran out of room in the barn. I bought a 15,000 sq. ft. building in Fishkill and moved West Tech. There was a new job in the works with Literly Laboratory in Suffern, New York. The construction manager was Tourcon Corporation. We had been doing a lot of work with them through the McBride Corporation. It would've been a perfect job to bid as prime air, so I set up a meeting with them to discuss the possibility of bidding it directly to them. I told them about the job I was doing with Whiting Turner at IBM as a prime contractor, and if they wanted to check with them, it would be fine with me. I explained to them how it would work. They said they would get back to me…the bid was years in the making. We had done a tremendous amount of work to make sure we were ready for this shift.

I called Joe McBride for a meeting to tell him what I was planning; I didn't want there to be any surprises for him. I figured he would be extremely mad at me for doing that, but it was what I needed to do for my company. We met, and he wasn't a happy camper, but he understood when I finished talking with him. From then on, whenever I could, I would bid for large jobs as a prime air job. If a mechanical contractor won that job, including the air side, I'd go back to them with a bid for the sheet metal side. Even when they didn't want to give me the job, they still did since I was the largest local contractor who could handle it. Nobody from out of town could beat my prices. If one of my competitors won the job, I would go back to them to see if they wanted me to do the drafting or fabrication. My nickname became "No Bottom Joe". They knew if I wanted the job, I would get it. When my number was at their cost, I still had a 10% profit on top of it.

By 1994, all three of my companies were running on all cylinders. Elmsford Sheet Metal was on track to hit 14 million in sales that year. WesTect would break 2 million in sales. East Coast had settled a lawsuit for patent infringement and was now creating new programs. The next half of the 90s were looking better than the first half.

***

I had a customer from Seattle who bought software from the East Coast. Meet Jerry Hermanson. He came from the same roots that I did. He was a sheet metal worker. When all the work broke out in Alaska on the pipeline, he went to work there and made plenty of money. When he came back to Seattle, he opened his own sheet metal shop. By the time I met him, he was well established as one of the larger contractors in the area. We had a lot in common and became good friends. He was quite the fisherman; he owned an island in Alaska where he did most of his fishing. One year, he called me up and told me he was going on a fishing expedition in Alaska at a camp. He invited a friend and me to join him. I took my salesman John Polaski with me because he loved fishing. We flew into a remote camp where he met us with several people who worked for him. There were two men and a guide to each boat. We had to be up by 430 a.m. for breakfast.

The first morning, we were sitting there having breakfast, and Jerry said to me,

"Hundred bucks for whoever brings in the biggest fish."

"Sure, I can beat you," I said.

When we got to the boat, he took out his fishing pole; it was 14 karat gold. I knew I was going to lose, and of course, I did. The next morning was the same thing; up at 4:30 for breakfast, and he said, "Double or nothing?" of course, I say yes. I don't think I have to say who brought in the biggest fish. The third morning, the same thing. Double or nothing, again. I was in for another loss. That night at dinner, I said to Jerry,

"I know you need another CAD system. Tomorrow's the last day so let's make a real bet." Everybody sitting at our table wanted to hear this one. I said, "A CAD station goes for 39,000 dollars. I'll make the following bet: if you win, I'll sell it to you for 34,000 dollars. If I win, you buy it for 44,000 dollars. That's a 10,000 dollars bet on the biggest fish." He said he would let me know in the morning.

We had our typical breakfast at 4:30. He turned to me and nodded his head. A simple yes to keep things interesting. I jumped up from the table and said to John, "Let's go, let's go, we have to get the biggest fish." We ran to the boat with our guide and jumped on board. When we were out of sight from the other boats, I told the guide to take us to town and that we needed breakfast. The guide said, "That's crazy, you have to win this bet!" I told the kid that it was going to be a lesson for him to take home. "I can't win this bet. He's never going to pay me 44,000 dollars for my product, so I need to lose the bet in order to make a 34,000 dollar sale." When we got back that night, we were both sitting in the boat, and everybody was waiting to see our fish. Jerry pulled out his fish. It was barely legal; it was the smallest fish he caught all week. Everybody thought I won, but I pulled up my pole, and I had nothing. I lost the bet, but I won the sale. Every year we would do a large computer show somewhere in the country, and every year Jerry would walk up to my booth, take out a 100 dollar bill and challenge me to liar's poker. (That's a poker game where numbers are used on paper money and try to bluff your opponent); it went on for years. I met a lot of great people in the business.

CHAPTER XXII

What Am I Going To Do With

A Freaking Island?

There was a lot of consolidation with construction companies going on in the late 90s. I was approached by a company called Emcor to meet with them over lunch about possibly being purchased. I met with them and listened to their sales pitch. At the end of the pitch, the guy said to me,

"You know, we don't write you a check for this. We let you have all the receivables that you earned up to now, then we give you a job."

"Cash will work," I said.

"No, you don't understand."

"Let me understand this. My company is making 14 million dollars a year in sales. I'm playing a hundred rounds of golf a year and you want me to give you my company so I can work for you? Well, thanks for lunch." I left with no deal. Around the same time, my wife and I bought an investment house on the lake, just around the corner from our home. We spent about a year renovating the inside and outside of the house. By the time we put the house on the market for sale, the market had fallen apart. We rented the house when we couldn't sell it. I definitely didn't want to be a landlord.

In 1994, towards the end of the summer, I was on my boat on Lake Mahopac with a few of my friends. We were driving by Petra Island, and I said, "I think I'll buy that island." We all laughed. A friend of mine, Dennis Holladay, was friends with the owner of the island. My wife and I, and Dennis and his wife Maryann, had gone out there for lunch one day. There was a cottage on the island that was built by the famous architect Frank Lloyd Wright. I was not too familiar with Frank Lloyd Wright at the time, and I didn't think much about it aside from its beauty. I went out there one other time when there was a group of people trying to raise money to build the original house that Frank Lloyd Wright also designed for the island. The owner had drawings of a house that was designed but never built. Over the winter, I heard there was a new owner on the island who was in financial trouble.

When the spring rolled around, early in May, I wrote up a note saying I was interested in purchasing the island. I put the note in a plastic sandwich bag, got on my wave runner, and went to the island. For as long as I could remember, the island was said to be guarded by two vicious dogs, and if you got anywhere near the island, they would come out in the water to get you. I took my wave runner up to the dock; I had a roll of duct tape with me, and I taped my note to the fence. Sure enough, the dogs came running. I jumped on the wave runner and took off, leaving my roll of duct tape on the dock. Every week or so, I would ride around the island and see my note still taped to the anchor fence. I knew somebody was around because somebody was feeding the dogs.

One day in June, I was on my wave runner riding by the island again, and I saw a man standing on the dock. I pulled up and introduced myself. His name was Mr. Park. He was from North Korea, and I had trouble understanding him. I said to him,

"I'm interested in buying your island."

"It definitely was for sale."

"I have a house on the lake, maybe we can trade the house and some cash for the island."

He said he might be interested in that. I asked if he would like to see the house, but he was flying back to California in the morning. He owned a tofu food factory there. I asked him if he would like to see the house right then, and he said yes! I could not take him to see the house on my wave runner, so I told him I would run home to get my boat and come back to pick him up. I jumped on my wave runner, and on the way back to my house, I stopped at the rented house to tell the people we had somebody coming to look at the house. When I got home, I said to my wife,

"Get on the boat, we are going to go buy an island."

"You're kidding," she said.

"No, I'm not! Let's go!"

We picked the island's owner up at the dock, as discussed earlier, and took him to the rented house. As he was looking around the house, he was complaining about things he didn't like. My wife thought he didn't like the house, but I told her he was trying to negotiate. When he was finished looking, we went back to the boat, and I realized we didn't have a pen or paper to exchange information with. I suggested we drive back to my house, and my wife would get us a pen and a piece of paper. We pulled up to my dock. My wife got out and went into the house. By the time she came back, we had a deal. We bought the island. My wife stayed at the house when I took him back to the island. As I was driving back home by myself, I said out loud, "What the hell did I just do? What the hell am I going to do with a freaking island?"

My friend Dennis Holiday had been on the island quite a bit over the years. I picked him up for dinner one night to pick his brain about a few things. We were on our way to the restaurant when I mentioned to him that I would need a piece of property for a dock to get to the island. He told me the island already had a dock right in town. We drove over to where he thought the dock was, and sure enough, there was a small dock right in the center of town. Mr. Park did not mention it, but that was no surprise since we only talked for 20 minutes before I purchased the island.

A couple of weeks later, I went to the closing with my lawyer, Mr. Park, and his lawyer. As we started going over the paperwork, I said to Mr. Park,

"I do not see the dock in town listed here."

"I'm not including the dock in town in the sale."

"The deal is off then," and got up to walk out.

Mr. Park stopped me before I reached the door and agreed to include the dock. To this day, I still don't know why he wanted to keep it. It was a small piece of land in town, and it belonged to the island. The total deal came down to trading the house, which I was glad to get rid of, and 300,000 dollars. After the closing, Mr. Park told me a story of why he had to sell the island to me. He explained, "There was a fable in North Korea, and it went like this. 'A master said to his slave, go out and find me a wife. The slave said, Master... how am I going to know what woman I should pick for your wife? The Master said, you will know when you find her. The slave went through the countryside for weeks, and one day, there were five or six women around the watering well. He was dirty from his travels through the countryside, and when he walked up to the well to get a drink of water, all the women but one backed away from him. He knew that the one woman who gave him water should be his master's wife.'" He continued, "I was a North Korean soldier, and I hated it. I wanted out of there. One day, a woman was nice to me when I was in the field. I knew that was my sign, and I walked out of North Korea through seven checkpoints, and nobody ever stopped me.

In North Korea, the white pig is sacred. When I saw your wife for the first time, I noticed she was so light-skinned. So I knew that was a sign that you were the people I had to sell the island to." I asked him how he ended up with an island in New York when his business was in California. He told me he got involved with the people who told him a Japanese firm was going to build the house that Frank Lloyd Wright designed on the island. He made an investment, and after a while, they told them they needed more money, and he gave it to them. Then, they told him that the deal fell apart and they would not build the house. He had so much invested in the deal that the other guys walked away from the island and gave it to him. He had three mortgages on the island, paying 10,000 dollars a month in interest. He needed that amount of cash to pay off his loans. He mortgaged the house he got in the trade, took the money, and headed back to California. You never know what deal is going to come your way. Most people don't even notice there is a deal staring them right in the face. And sometimes, even when they know it's a good deal, they can't pull the trigger. A lot of people would think that sometimes I'm too fast on the trigger. Not all my deals have been good, but I have a great average.

After the closing of the deal, I took my boat and went out to the island. It was the first time I stepped on the island in years. When I used to waterski around it as a kid, the thought about ever owning the island had never entered my mind. I walked into the cottage and started checking things out. It was obvious that no one had been living there; there was only one lightbulb working in the whole cottage. They suckered that poor guy in. I started making mental notes of what I needed to do to fix the place up. I never really had any interest in Frank Lloyd Wright's work, but as I looked around the cottage, I started to realize that it was pretty amazing. It was entirely constructed of redwood, concrete, and rock. That little cottage was 900 square feet, but with the wide-open floor plan and the large windows, it felt like I was outside. The cottage was 45 years old when I purchased it. The floor was red concrete with a triangular pattern.

I noticed all the walls were laid out on top of the triangular pattern. There were two fireplaces back to back; one was meant to heat the master bedroom when the door was closed, and the other to heat the living space. The master bedroom was separated from the living room with accordion-type redwood doors. They were supposed to fold into each other and be completely out of the way when open, to appear as one large room. They were not in good shape; I thought fixing them would be a good project for me over the winter. I would take them completely apart and refinish them at my house. In the spring, I would bring them back and reinstall them. The roof was a cedar shake and in need of repair. Otherwise, the cottage was in great shape. The island was 10.8 acres with a beautiful walking trail around its perimeter. It was time to explore the island itself. It was about a three-quarter mile walk around the perimeter and with completely different views of the lake as you move around the island. The island, in the center, rose over 100 feet from the water. It really was a special place. I was very happy with my purchase.

***

I was the president of the Local Contractors Association. I'd been dealing with the Union president, Charlie Hertel, for the last ten years. We had a very good relationship and got along well. The president of the Union before Charlie was very hard to work with… most of them were. Charlie told me that he was looking to retire. His executive vice president was Gino Colombo. I worked with Gino on labor management, but I didn't know him very well. His brother Nikki Colombo was a business agent with the Union. I heard there was some turmoil going on between the Colombo's and Charlie Hertel. It was basically about who was going to be the next president of the local Union.

I invited the three of them to come out to the island where they could work out their problems without any outside influence. We all went out to the island on a cool April day. I just picked up a broom and started sweeping while they got into their conversation. When things got heated, I would interject a little something into their conversation, and they would continue. I could tell that both Gino and Nicky were hotheads. Charlie, on the other hand, was mild as you could be. At one point, Nicky got mad at something and went out for a walk. I said to Nicky, "Where are you going, Nicky? You are on an island, there is no place to go!" He went back in, and after a while, they resolved the issues.

In 1996, Gino became president of the Union. I was not sure I was happy with it; I had no idea how he was going to be like to work with. 1996 was the best year my company ever had. We exceeded 18 million dollars in sales. The rest of the 90s looked to be even better. I was still president of the Local Association, president of the Local Joint Adjustment Board, and president of the Upcoming Local Negotiations. I was also on the National Labour Relations Board and was elected as a board member of The Sheet Metal Contractors International. I had a little problem with Gino as president of the Local Union. I appointed one of my employees to become the apprentice teacher. At one point, Gino fired him and put his own man in charge. It didn't sit well with me, but there was not much I could do about it.

***

At the end of 1998, I was in negotiations with the large distribution center for Old Navy. Part of my pitch to them was that I had a very good relationship with the Union, which meant they would not have any Union problems from my end on the project. I was not happy with the Union representative that Gino put in charge of the project. I told Gino the guy would get him in trouble, but he said he would be just fine. About three-quarters of the way through the project, I was at the airport waiting for a connecting flight when my phone rang. It was the guy I negotiated the Old Navy job with. He said to me,

"Hey, Joe… How are you? How's everything going?"

"Good, how about you?"

"How's that relationship going that you have with the Union?"

"Good, why? What's going on?"

"If your relationship is so good then maybe you could explain to me why 20 of your men are outside surrounding the truck trying to make a delivery here."

Once I got my blood pressure down a point or two, I said to him, "I'll take care of it."

I called the Union hall and said, "I want to speak with Gino Colombo, this is Joe Massaro!"

"Oh, sorry Joe, he's not in right now."

In the old days, when there was a problem on the job site, and it was a Union demonstration, you could never get a hold of the president; he would conveniently disappear until the problem went away. I told her to tell Gino to get on the phone now. She said he wasn't there. I said, "You tell him to call me as soon he comes in."

About 20 minutes later, my phone rang. It was Gino. He said to me,

"What's up Joe?" as if he had no idea why I was calling, so I let him have it.

"What's up? You know what's up, don't play games with me. There are 20 men surrounding the trucks on the Old Navy project."

"Joe I don't know anything about that."

"Gino, don't give me that BS. Either you are lying to me or you are the dumbest president of the Union I have ever seen. How could you not know what's going on?"

"I swear to you I don't know what's going on, but I will find out."

He called me back 20 minutes later and told me the truck was released. I told him I was bringing him up on charges for his negligence.

He responded, "I'll meet you on the job first thing in the morning and we will find out together what is going on."

The next morning I was still smoking hot. When I saw Gino, I told him I was filing charges against the Union for the illegal work stoppage. He said, "I want to settle this under step one." Step one is a Union process where you can resolve the problem right on the spot without kicking it up to a higher level. He asked what I wanted from him in order to make it right. I said,

"The first thing I want is for you to pay my men who I had to dock for being off the job, then I want your idiot business agent off the job site."

"Okay I'll take over this job myself. Anything else?"

"No, that'll do."

Then he said to me, "I want to meet the guy who called you and apologize to him for my guys' actions."

I looked at him and said, "Gino, you don't have to do that."

"Yes, I do," and that's what he did.

We became friends after that. In 1999, Gino and I negotiated a ten-year Union contract for our area with money in it every year. This was unheard of in our industry. Most Union contracts were a maximum of three years. It was groundbreaking. It gave stability to the industry in our area. Otherwise, every two to three years, we would be threatened with a strike. Gino and I clearly worked well together. It was the beginning of a successful Union relationship and a lifelong friendship.

CHAPTER XXIII

Getting My Chips Off The Table

In 1999, I started looking for ways to reduce my risk. The companies were in the best shape of their lives. We had more than five years of solid, certified statements and a 7 million dollar line of credit with the bank, along well as a 50 million dollar bonding capability. There was a lot of consolidation going on in the industry. It looked like a prime time to get serious. Frank Candela, my joint venture partner from McBride, had been on sabbatical for about a year. I called him up and asked him if he was bored yet. He asked me what I had in mind. I told him I needed him to do all the paperwork that was going to be required for me to sell my business. That's what Frank was an expert at; paperwork was not my strength. Frank came on board, and we started to process.

***

The year 2000 was my best and worst year. We landed a 23 million dollars job at IBM Fishkill, which was my company's largest job yet. But on a personal level, 2000 was the year that I lost my best cheerleader, my mom. Every time I landed a big job throughout my career, I would stop by to see her and say, "Hey, Mom, look what your dumb kid did now." My mom didn't think I was dumb. Still, compared to my brother, the Aeronautical

219

engineer, and my sister, the lawyer, I was the only one without a college education, so I liked to brag to my mom about all the things I accomplished without spending all that money on college. My brother was in California, and my sister was in Denver, so it was up to me to take care of my mother, who lived alone in Elmsford. Whenever we went on a family vacation, my mother came with us. We spent every holiday with her. She spent every New Year's Eve with my girls so Barbara and I could have some fun together. She was a very important part of all of our lives.

As she got older and her health was declining, she asked me to take her to the lawyer so she could set up a living will. I set up a meeting with my lawyer, and we went to his office to sign the papers. As they slid the papers over to her to sign, she said to me, "Joseph, there is just one thing I need to clarify. If you are going to pull the plug on me, before you do it, I want you to come over and whisper in my ear. If you see my middle finger go up don't pull the plug!" So, of course, eventually, I got the call that she was in the emergency room on life support. I rushed down there and met with the doctor, who was a friend of hers. He said to me, "I know she doesn't want to be on life support, but I think we can help her." I went in to see her. She was lying in the fetal position. Her eyes fluttered open when I walked over, and her middle finger came up a little bit. She lived another year after that; she got to see my youngest daughter get married and meet her first great grandchild.

When she was in hospice, my oldest daughter Donna and I took her oxygen and a wheelchair and put it in the car to take her to the casino. She always loved the casino.

She said, "Joseph, I can't do this. I am on hospice."

I said, "Mom, what are they going to do, throw you out?"

During the last year of her life, she did get thrown out of hospice several times! Not because of that casino trip, but because she was a fighter. She refused to move in with my family because she was determined to stay in her own home, so I hired a 24 hour-in home care for her. She got to see my success; that was good for her and me. She died in her own home. I miss her dearly.

***

We had been doing some work in Connecticut with the HT Lions Corporation. Pennsylvania Power and Light recently purchased them. They were looking to expand in our area where all the IBM work was. We sent them our brochure that Frank put together. Our sales pitch was for them to purchase our company, and I would stay on to run it along with any other sheet metal companies they purchased. A couple of months later, the president of HT Lyons came down to speak to me about a potential purchase. He said they were interested in both Elmsford Sheet Metal and West Tech International, but they didn't want me! Just my companies. They didn't think I was corporate material. I said,

"You mean you're going to give me a check and I just walk out?"

"Yep, that's what they want to do."

He gave me an offer right then and there! I had been working since I was 17 years old. The most time I could get off from work was the ten days I took for Thanksgiving week. I only missed three days of work for that each year because the other days were either holiday or weekend. Later on, if I could get a week at a time, that would be a lot. In 1997 we decided to rent a place in Florida for three months in the winter. It was a nice house on the intercostal. It had an orange and a grapefruit tree in the yard. I spent two weeks there but had to go back to work; the downtime was killing me. The next year, we rented a three-story townhouse right on Juno Beach, Florida. It was a beautiful place; I almost got three weeks in before I went stir crazy.

In the spring of 1999, my wife called to rent the same townhouse for that season. I was at the golf course having lunch when she called me all upset and said the condo we wanted was already rented to someone else for the season. I thought it would be fine to rent a different place, but my wife was set on the same one. She said, "I'm going to call them and see if they want to sell the place." I was pretty sure nothing would come of it, but she called me back and said it wasn't for sale, but if we wanted to pay 500,000 dollars, it could be. I called the guy up and told him I would give him 450,000 dollars. He said 500,000 dollars or nothing, so we bought it. He went around bragging to everybody about how much he got for his townhouse. He must've bought it in the 80s when it was first built. He probably paid less than 100,000 dollars for it. One year later, it was worth 1.2 million dollars.

Back to the meeting, I was wrestling with this decision about selling my companies and walking away. A construction company was not very easy to sell. The construction business runs hot and cold with the economy. One day you could be knocking them dead, and the next day you're sitting with big overhead and no work. The offer on the table was very decent. I called up HT Lyons and told them I was interested in selling, but the number they gave me was too low. With the IBM job I landed at 23 million dollars, and the other work I had on hand, they would have to sweeten the offer. They sweetened their offer, but they wanted some assurance that the profits estimates were accurate. I told them that I would guarantee that my two companies would make a gross profit of 4 million dollars each year for three years. They could hold back 1 million dollars of the sale price, but any profits over 4 million dollars per year I wanted 50% of. I was only hoping to get 10%, but they agreed to the deal. They figured there was no way this company had that kind of profits. I put Frank Candela in charge of all the paperwork that had to be done; there was a ton of it. It took him weeks to put everything together. Finally, we were done and ready for the closing.

The closing was to be held at Fishkill in the Marriott hotel. I was dealing with Pennsylvania Power and Light; they were a bunch of serious, straight-laced guys. I walked into a big conference room with my lawyer; there was a long table with all the paperwork on it and probably eight lawyers on their side, plus management. I walked in, looked around; everybody was quiet, and I said, "You know what guys, I don't think I go through with this." I never saw so many people turn white. Before they got really crazy, I told them I was only kidding. I signed the papers, and I was out of a job, just like that.

A few nights later, we had a dinner with all my key personnel and top management from PP&L to introduce everybody and tell them what was going on (which they kind of already knew— it's hard to keep gossip out of the shop). I knew my guys were sorry to see me go. An offer like that only comes through once in a lifetime, and you have to know when to pull the trigger. My employees knew I cared about them, and most of them liked working for me. Our turnover rate was still at zero. This meeting reminded me of the scene in that old show M.A.S.H.; when radar was leaving, he looked into the operating room window, and everything was going on just like when he was there. That's kind of the feeling I had. I had 300 men working for me at the time. I had to give up all the committees that I worked on, I had to leave my men in the hands of strangers, and I had to let go of the business I grew for the last 20 years. It was like leaving a part of myself behind, but it would all still go on without me.

***

By the end of the first year, the company was at 16 million dollars in profits. I went back to them and told them I met my obligation and I wanted my million dollars released. They complained that the deal was to release the money at the end of three years. I told them I had no control over how they ran their company over the next two years. I wanted my money now. They still refused, so I had my lawyer send them a letter. After a few weeks of negotiations, they cut me a large check for 50% of the profits; they made over 12 million dollars. They were not happy campers. A year after I left, the company went from 300 employees to less than 50. They took two vibrant companies and ran them into the ground. But they said they didn't want me to run their company because I was not "corporate material." Both companies closed their doors in 2019. I wonder what their definition of "corporate material" is now?

CHAPTER XXIV

What The Hell Am I Going To Do Now?

I bought a brand-new 2001 Mercedes Coupè SL 500 and headed down to Florida all by myself. I had the top down and took all the back roads; I was in no rush for the first time in my life. The phone had not rung since I left. Just a few weeks ago, I had two phones with one in each ear. I had meetings to go to, fires to put out, and now... nothing. I stopped at small restaurants along the way. When I got tired, I got a hotel room. It took me four days to get to my place in Juno beach. When I got there, I took my beach chair, my towel, a book, and planted myself on the beach for the next few days, giving myself some time to clear my head. I was not wondering if I did the right thing. I knew I did. The question was... where do I go from here?

One day, I took my bicycle to the grocery store. I saw a woman and her daughter struggling to change a flat tire on her Rent-A-Car. They had no idea what they were doing. They were trying to take a hubcap off where there was no hubcap. So I went over and helped them change a tire. When I was finished, I asked them if they had a rag so I could clean my hands. She gave me a rag and then tried to give me a 20 dollar bill for helping her. I had a laugh and said, "Lady, I don't want your 20 dollars. Two weeks ago I sold my company for millions of dollars, it was my pleasure to help you," and I got back on my bike and peddled back to the beach. I think my mom would have been proud.

I still had my computer company East Coast Sheet Metal. In 1982 we had developed our first plasma cutting system for L-tec with that "portable" computer from I.B.M. After the success we had at that first show, we had a lot more programming to do, and Jerry could not do it alone. Since Jerry was from New York City and that was where we could get good programmers from back then, we rented an office on 16th St. in downtown New York City and started building our programming staff. We needed to develop a program for round duct next. L-tac had salesmen all over the United States. The problem was they were not true salesmen; they were order takers. The only thing they were good for was getting us leads, but we had to do the real work to close the deals. If we could get the leads to the shop to see our machine in action, we had a 95% close rate.

In the early 80s, we had the duct fabrication program running pretty well. Combining that program with the L-tech plasma cutting system gave us the most powerful system out there. The biggest difference was that the software was written by a sheet metal contractor using programmers. The other systems were written by engineers who didn't know that much about sheet metal, so we had a real advantage over the shops around the country. We knew how to read, write and speak shop. My next step was to start looking into automating my drafting department. If I could develop a Computer-Aided Design (CAD) system that could draw ductwork and then automatically create the shop ticket and send it to the plasma cutting systems, that would change the industry.

I went to the CAD show in New York City to see what was available. There were several systems that architects used to develop drawings. I was interested in two of them. One was AutoCAD, which was a new company. The other one I looked at was a product called I-Draw. I brought Jerry with me to the show to look at both systems. We selected AutoCAD and purchased it. A few days later, we had the system in-house, and Jerry started looking into it. I got a call from the salesman at I-Draw; he was in the area and wanted to come up and show me the difference between AutoCAD and I-DRAW. I told him we already started working on AutoCAD, but he insisted on having just 15 minutes in my office. The next day, he came up with his programmer and compared his product and AutoCad. There was no comparison.

The I-Draw product was much easier to use and much faster. I was building this system mainly for my own shop. We made the change and developed our program on I-DRAW. The computer we used was Vector Automation; it was a large computer similar in size to my Burroughs Computer. We developed a 2-D cad/cam system that one could use to draw rectangular and round ducts, and we downloaded it to my duct fabrication program. We called the program EC CAD. In my building, where we housed Elmsford Sheet Metal, we built a new CAD drafting room and installed six new Vector computers with our software on them for drawing and fabricating ductwork. The room looked like no other drafting room for sheet metal drafting. Instead of drafting boards and T squares, we had computerized workstations. All of our drawings were now done on the new 2D cad. We used that room as a showroom to bring potential customers in as well. The computers were so large that we had to move them by forklift. The sale price for one computer system, including hardware and software, was 105,000 dollars. Over the next couple of years, we sold about ten systems. The technology was moving real fast. By 1985 we were able to move our system from a big workstation like Vector Automation to a personal computer like IBM.

I wanted to rewrite the program in 3-D; I still had my office in New York City with about six programmers. My top programmer Jerry was a little burnt out at this point. He wanted to move on to do something else. I interviewed a couple of new programmers to take the top position, and the one I selected was a Russian guy named Vladimír. He reshaped the program department and changed all my programs to "windows based". Now we had a portable CAD system, and we lowered the price of the CAD product to 39,000 dollars. I bought a small truck and set the truck up with my CAD\CAM products right on board. I sent the truck across the country, demonstrating the software products right at the customer shops. One of my salesmen would drive the truck to a city, do demonstrations, then leave the truck at the airport and fly back. My other salesman would fly to that airport, pick up the truck, and head to the next city. We were doing okay with this method and started thinking about putting another truck on the road.

I was doing a show in Toronto with our CAD system. During one of my demonstrations on the new CAD product, I noticed a man standing behind me watching the demo. I recognized him; his name was Curtis Brockton. He was president of a company called Quick Pen International. What they had was a computerized estimating system for sheet metal, piping, and plumbing contractors. The system was pretty well-known. When I finished my demonstration, Curtis said to me, "Your system looks very good, how many trucks do you have on the road. I see them in every airport."

I laughed and gave him a personal demonstration of our product. At the end of it, I said to him, "Are you interested in selling this product for me?"

He said, "Yes".

Quick Pen had about six salesmen across the country. Our CAD/CAM product was a natural fit with their product. We made a deal making Quick Pen the official sales agent for East Coast CAD/CAM. This arrangement ended around 1992 after we were sued for patent infringement from a company called Construction Technology. There were about six companies in total that were sued.

We all met in an office in New York City. I walked into that meeting with six companies and six different lawyers. I thought that was crazy. We should've had one lawyer only for the six companies. Of course, they claimed conflict of interest couldn't be done. I knew we were in trouble, but once Construction Technology beat the first company, which was the Lock Former Company, in court, there wasn't much we could do. In court, they proved that the LockFormer Company had stolen a piece of paper from Construction Technology. Legally, we thought we were clean because it was proven that Construction Technology sold a system one year prior to any patent. That should've automatically killed the patent. But with the jury finding that they stole the piece of paper, Lock Former lost the case. I was the last one they sued. I actually had developed my product at the same time they did. I thought I had a better case than everybody else.

The problem was everybody else was starting to settle with them. I tried fighting a little while longer. We were spending hundreds of thousands on lawyers. We knew we had to settle; I was hung up on one part of the deal. We were called into federal court to explain to the judge why we would not comply with the patent. My lawyer gave the argument to the judge, and the judge said to my lawyer, "The next time your client comes into my courtroom, tell him to bring his toothbrush." I turned to my lawyer and said it's time to settle. By the time we finished with the lawyers and the settlement, it cost me nearly 1 million dollars. It happened one year after I purchased the business from Vincent. Theoretically, he was liable for half of it. I didn't bother going after him for that. Part of the settlement was that I had to pay Construction Technology 10,000 dollars in royalties for every program I sold. The patent was good for another eight years.

***

In the early 90's when Russia opened up its market to America, my programmer Vladimír made arrangements for us to meet with businessmen in Moscow. I had to fly to England, so I made arrangements to meet Vladimír in Moscow a few days later. I got to fly to England on the supersonic concorde. What an amazing flight that was; two times the speed of sound. When in Moscow, I stayed at a hotel in Red Square. The next morning we met with about 12 businessmen from Moscow. We were seated at a long table at about 8 o'clock in the morning. The door opened and a Russian woman with a silver tray that had cognac and vodka on it, came in. I said to Vladimír, "This is not a bad way to start a meeting." These businessmen had some items that they wanted to see if there was a market in the States for. One was a fencing sword that when the tip broke off it would break off flat without a point. I had no interest in that. They went to several other items that didn't sound too interesting. Then they came up with a television screen that produced no X-rays from the screen. I did not know if that was a big deal or not, but my brother was big into manufacturing computer parts. That night, I called him and asked if he thought that had any value. He said that if indeed it had no X-rays coming out of it, it could be very important.

The next morning, we were at another meeting with them and I told them we were interested in looking at the TV. They were going to make arrangements to take me to the lab where the TV located. At the meeting, a young boy was sitting at the table and Vladimír said to me, "That is the son of the boss, he's a programmer." I said to Vladimír, "Hire him." His name was Elia. That afternoon, they took me to a clean room where the TV was. The IBM clean rooms I worked in America were very sophisticated. You had to be fully covered in head to toe clothing, boots, mask, and through an air chamber to get inside. In Moscow, the clean room consisted of pieces of plastic hanging down at the door entrance!

I looked at the TVs and we made arrangements to ship them back to the States for testing. I then invited a few of them to come to America. I learned a few things in Russia; when the driver would stop and get out of the car he would take his windshield wipers with him. Apparently, they stole windshield wipers off of cars. The other thing I noticed was how pretty the women were. I was used to seeing them on television with the Russian women looking like peasants. In Moscow, there were beautiful Russian women everywhere.

About a week later, the top Russians from Moscow came to New York. I showed them around my shop and went to lunch at one of my favorite restaurants. They were famous for their prime rib and that's what we ordered. When they came out, the prime rib was hanging over the dish; their eyes were wide open like they couldn't believe what they were seeing. I don't think they had ever seen a piece of meat like that. The next place I took them was to a supermarket. Again, they could not believe their eyes. We were doing a sheet-metal project at a can manufacturing company not far from my shop. Packaging was one of Russia's problems. A can manufacturer was producing millions of cans a day and blew the Russians away. After all that, it turned out they could not get their TVs out of Russia. I ended up with Elia. He became an American citizen and a fantastic programmer who ended up heading up my programming staff in Russia for years to come.

***

In 1998, I brought my new son-in-law on board with me at East Coast Sheet Metal. Meet Dave; he graduated from college as an engineer, married my youngest daughter Jennifer, and had my first grandson, Jake. After the patent problem, L-tech wanted to separate their company from the duct cutting business. I decided it was time for us to build our own plasma cutting system. That's what I hired Dave for. While sitting on the beach for two weeks after I sold my company, I figured it was time for me to go back and do something. I needed a new place to house my software company and someplace to build the new plasma cutter.

I found a perfect building in Fishkill, New York, about 20 miles from my old shop. I bought the building and duplicated my old office into the new building. I used the same desk, the same pictures on the wall, and some of the same staff. I made Frank Candela my new chief operating officer. I hired my daughter Donna for the ninth time in her life as my new office manager. She had an interesting track record. When she worked at my other company, she would call in dead if she was out of sick days! She was getting a little older though, and she promised she wouldn't quit for at least a year. I put my salesman John Polaski, who used to be a machinist, in charge of building the new plasma tables in the new building. We hired a new marketing manager, and Frank put a whole new business plan together. The construction technologies patent was going to end in a couple of years, and I wanted to be ready to take back the industry.

***

At the beginning of 2003, I was totally bored. I didn't want to spend any time in my office anymore. Everybody was doing their job at East Coast; they only needed me as a consultant. I needed more action! I used to run companies that had 300 people working for me. I called Dave and told him I was going to make him my partner and eventually president... and that we were moving the business up to Boston, where he lived. He had been running most of it up to now anyway. I sold the building and moved the operations to Boston.

CHAPTER XXV

Doubling Down On A Bad Deal

(Lake Placid)

My friend from Lake Placid, Mike Nicole, called me; he wanted to present me with a deal. You remember Mike? He owned the pizza shop that I put my trailer behind to sell tickets at the Olympics. I first met Mike when he was a bartender at the Dew Drop Inn. It was an Italian restaurant in Saranac Lake, which is about 20 miles from Lake Placid. I remember when he went to Lake Placid and opened a very small pizza place. He didn't even have the machines needed to make the dough. From that pizza place, he and his brother were able to open a large pizzeria right on Main Street in Lake Placid. Every restaurant Mike owned was profitable.

He was a very good businessman and had a great personality. While he still owned 50% of the pizza shop that his brother was running, Mike opened a restaurant in Lake Placid, a nice steak restaurant. He was leasing the building. After that lease ran out, he opened an Italian restaurant called Nicole's Over Main Street. Whenever I went to Lake Placid, I ate at his restaurants. They were very successful restaurants. His new restaurant had about 100 seats and always had a line out the door.

I headed up to Lake Placid to meet Michael. We met at his restaurant. He told me his dream was to build a new restaurant and a small hotel on Main St. in Lake Placid. There was a piece of property coming up for sale right across from the Olympic Arena, and a couple of other pieces of property near there were probably coming up for auction soon. He took out a preliminary plan he had for the new restaurant. He was proposing to create two restaurants in one, with an Italian restaurant on one side and a steak and seafood on the other. It was a 15,000 sq. ft. building with a larger room upstairs to be used for weddings and catering.

He had prepared a business plan, showing the possible revenues that the restaurant could provide. It would be a two-phase plan. He would build the restaurant first and then decide if we wanted to build the hotel. There were a lot of restaurants in Lake Placid, but not one like he was suggesting. There used to be a restaurant in Lake Placid called the Steak and Stinger. It was a very popular restaurant, and it always had a waiting list to get in. The owner got in trouble someplace and lost the restaurant. Lake Placid was a very seasonal location with the summer and ski seasons.

Mike and I took a ride down to where the property was. It was directly across the street from the old Olympic arena. There was an old house sitting on top of the hill that was the main piece of the property. The other two pieces of property were behind, on the backside street. I looked at the hill that the house was sitting on, and I said to Mike,

"We have to take this mountain out of here."

"Joe, I found out that mountain is nothing but dirt that came from the basement of the old Olympic arena when they built it for the 1936 Olympics. I found a guy who would remove it and take it away for the fill."

The other two pieces of property were coming up for an auction; they should be very reasonable. I asked Mike how I fit into his plan, he said, "I want you as a partner; it will be 50% on the building and the steak restaurant, and 30% on the Italian restaurant. You're familiar with the construction industry, so you can put the job together and oversee the plans and construction. I will need you to cosign the loan on the building, then at the end of five years I will buy you out of it."

"Mike, this is a big project. I have to think about if I really want to get involved."

While I was up there in the Adirondacks, I figured I might as well spend a couple of days. I gave my lawyer Charlie a call, and we met at the "cottage" for cocktails. I talked to him about what Mike wanted to do, and Charlie told me the same thing he told me before I did the Olympics. "Run, Joe, run. Didn't you have enough of Lake Placid yet?" I told him the business plan looked really good. "What could go wrong?" He just gave me "the look" and shook his head.

The next day, I rented a boat and went up to Eggplant's camp. When I told Eggplant the plan, he asked what kind of drugs I was on! I hadn't made my decision yet, but it was not because of these guys. People had been trying to talk me out of making deals for years. If I listened to them, I might've missed a bad deal here or there, but I also would've missed some really good deals; I could still be pumping gas if I never took Vincent's deal.

After a couple of days with Eggplant, I headed home to discuss the decision with my wife, who also thought I was crazy. One of the reasons I was interested in taking the deal was, I wanted to get even with Lake Placid after the Olympics. This could be a way of crossing off that loss on my resume. Watch out for trying to get even. A couple of days later, I called Mike and told him I was interested in the deal, but I wanted 50% of the Italian restaurant as well. I didn't want to try to figure out which restaurant was making money and which was losing money. He agreed with the deal.

The next thing we needed to do was buy the first piece of property. Michael had already negotiated with the owners and settled on a number. We met with the local bank and set up a construction loan which I backed-up with my financial statements and a personal guarantee. The next thing we did was buy the second piece of property before it went to auction. We tried to do that on the third piece of property, but somebody else bought it, thinking that we would pay a lot more for it. That other piece of property was not important for the restaurant, but possibly for the hotel, which I really had no interest in. We hired an architect who started to design the building. After the drawings were completed, we went out to bid. I sent a set of drawings to the heating and contractor in my area, a good friend who owned a sheet metal business since I had sold mine by then.

***

Meet Richard Lomas and Gregory Dopky. Richard and Greg owned a company named ABM Heating and Air Conditioning, which was a competitor of mine before I sold Elmsford Sheet Metal. We were friendly competitors, and because all three of us sat on the board of SMACNA, we traveled the world playing golf together for years. After I sold my company, whenever I needed HVAC work done, I would go to ABM.

Meet Andrew Young. Andrew was the president of our local golf club. As a career, he was a professional kitchen designer. Andrew had designed commercial kitchens for restaurants all over the world. Greg was a pilot and owned a small plane. Richard, Andrew, Greg, and I all flew up to Lake Placid to check out the building, layout the kitchen and the duct for the project.

I spent the next couple of years working on the project. I reviewed all the bids and selected the contractors. The construction phase of the project went very well, and in 2006 we had our grand opening. The building was a two-story brick building, and I was very happy with the outcome. For the next year and a half, the restaurant was performing like the business plan predicted. "What could possibly go wrong?" How about the financial crash of 2008? How about no snow for skiing that winter? Or an even a bigger crash that was worse than all my bad deals combined. Richard, Greg, Andrew, and I were members of the same golf club. Aside from traveling the world playing golf, the four of us played golf together every weekend.

We had our own table at the club that was reserved for our breakfast. We were a foursome to be reckoned with on the course and at the bar! Twice a year, fall and spring, the four of us would take Greg's small plane down to North Carolina, where Andrew was partners in a hotel to play golf. Sometimes, we would have two or three small planes full of players with us. I was usually Greg's copilot.

In March of 2007, my daughter Donna was living and working in Lake Tahoe. There was a big poker tournament in Reno I wanted to play in, so I planned a visit with Donna after the tournament. Instead of flying to North Carolina with Greg and the boys, I would fly commercially and meet them at a small airport in Pinehurst, North Carolina. It was a beautiful day on the fourth of April, 2007. In Pinehurst, five of us were waiting at the airport for

Greg's plane to land within the hour. Fred Willmont was a friend of ours; he provided all the woodwork for my Frank Loyd Wright's house. About an hour after they were scheduled to land, Fred got a call that the plane went down in a storm in Virginia. Greg, Richard, and Andrew were all gone, just like that on a sunny day when we were supposed to be golfing. We were in shock. The five of us were just walking around the airport terminal completely in shock. Bill Wedral, one of the five of us, lived near me in Florida and had his car there at the airport. He drove me back to Florida from North Carolina. It was one of the very worst times of my life. It was life-changing for me.

CHAPTER XXVI

What Are The Chances Of Building The Masterpiece

When I purchased Petra Island in 1995, I didn't plan on building the unbuilt Frank Lloyd Wright masterpiece. The thought never crossed my mind. I didn't even remember what the house looked like. Like most of the things I have done, I purchased the island first and would figure out what to do with it later. As far as I was concerned, it was a good deal mainly because I got rid of the other house I could not sell. I fell in love with the island pretty quickly. I had never been a detail-oriented guy. For some reason, that changed when I stepped on the island. The first thing I noticed was that the roof on the cottage needed to be replaced. It was a cedar shake roof, and it was 45 years old. I hired a contractor to do the work. The cedar shakes on the cottage were 18 inches long. The contractor told me he could only get 14-inch long cedar. I told him that was not acceptable. "Someone must make 18-inch cedar shakes, that's what I want."

He found the cedar shakes from a company in Canada. When we took off the old cedar roof, some of the cedar still had the company's name on it. It turned out to be the same company they purchased the material from 45 years earlier. I spent most of my weekends on the island fixing up the cottage. The cottage was in very good shape overall.

When we first purchased the island, we contacted the Frank Lloyd Wright Foundation to ask for copies of the original drawings for both the cottage and the original house that Frank designed but never built. When they got back to us, they said they did not have original drawings of either the cottage or the house. They only had 8.5 x 11-inch pictures of the drawings, and there were four drawings of the cottage and three drawings of the main house. We purchased these from the Frank Lloyd Wright Foundation.

When I received the drawings from the foundation, I could immediately see that the main house that was designed for the spot to be built was magnificent. The drawings were so small that it was really hard to see the details. I used a magnifying glass to see some of the drawing details, and then I redrew the house to full scale using my computer system. Before I built my other house on the lake, I built a scale model of it from the drawings I developed. It helped me see how the roof was going to fit onto the curved living room. I decided to build a scale model of the main house that Frank Lloyd Wright designed as his masterpiece. The model was set up in a way I could lift the roof off to see the interior. In the original drawing of the main house, they included the island's topographical contours with a big rock showing. With that drawing, I could lay out the house on the island on the exact spot

Frank Lloyd Wright had chosen. The more I looked at the house, the more intrigued I became.

***

A few years later, my wife called me and said she received a call from the marina on Lake Mahopac telling her that some guy wanted to rent a boat to go out and see the cottage on the island. She said she told the marina not to rent him a boat. A couple of days later, I received a telephone call from a guy who introduced himself as Tom Heinz, an Architect & Author from Chicago who also happened to be a Frank Lloyd Wright enthusiast. He told me that he had photographed every house that Frank Lloyd Wright ever built except the cottage and would really love to add pictures of the cottage to his collection. I told Tom I would be glad to take him out to the island. We set up a date, and I picked him up in my boat. He spent a few hours taking pictures of the cottage. He knew of the unbuilt house. He said it was in a couple of books he had seen over the years. He would try to get me a copy. About two weeks later, I received a package in the mail from Tom Heinz with copies of all the letters that went back-and-forth between Frank Loyd Wright and the owners of Petra Island during the construction of the cottage. I said to my wife, "See what happens when you are nice to people?"

***

In 1948, a man named Ahmed Chahroudi purchased Petra Island at auction. His sole reason for purchasing the island was to have Frank Lloyd Wright design a house for him. In 1949 he commissioned Frank Lloyd Wright to design a house for the island. He told Frank to "Design your masterpiece, and I will build it on the island." Frank had a free hand on this one. Without any input from the owner, he designed the 5000 sq. ft. house hanging over the lake, unlike any other house he ever designed. The ceilings were unusually high. There was a rock shaped like a breaching whale, which started outside the house and went right into the house through the dining room and back out the other side. The cantilever was twice that of the Fallingwater home. As a matter of fact, in one of the books that Tom had sent me, 'The Many Faces of Frank Lloyd Wright,' Frank said, "When I complete the house on the island, it will be more beautiful than my Fallingwater."

When Frank completed the drawings, Mr. Chahroudi met him in Arizona to view them. A few weeks after being back from Arizona, he contacted Mr. Wright and told him the house was too big for him and he didn't think he could afford it. Mr. Chahroudi also didn't think the town would give him the permits needed to build it. He asked Frank to design his guest cottage first. After he built that, the town might've been more amenable to let him build the big house. Frank Lloyd Wright designed the cottage for them. In one of the letters from Mrs. Chahroudi to Mr. Wright, he asked

Mr. Wright to switch the fees they had paid him for the big house with the design of the cottage. Mr. Wright's answer to that was, "I don't switch fees." The cottage was built in 1952. Frank Lloyd Wright visited the island to see the cottage while he was working on the Guggenheim Museum.

When I finally completed the house on the island, Mrs. Chahroudi was still alive; she told me her husband never intended to build the big house, and he just used that to get Frank to design his cottage. After I sold my Elmsford Sheet Metal and West Tech, and moved East Coast Sheet Metal to Boston, I started to get serious about looking into building the house. I was in the locker room of my golf course in Mahopac one day, and a member of my club, Bill Spain, was there. His father opened the original bank in our town. The family owned banks, oil companies, insurance companies, and legal offices in town. They had a lot of influence in our town. I asked Bill if he knew about the house that was designed on Petra Island that was never built, and he did. In fact, he was very familiar with it. When he was a boy, Bill told me he used to walk on the island and asked me if it would be okay if he stopped by and took a walk now and then. I said,

"Sure, Bill. Anytime you want to is okay with me. What do you think the chances are of the town letting me build that house out there?"

"Joe, there is an opening on the lake committee. I think it would be a really good place to start if you were on that committee to show you care about the lake. If I recommend you, will you go on the committee?"

"Sure!" I did love the lake, and I was retired; I needed some new hobbies.

He said to me, "Joe, I think you have a good chance of building that house on the island, good luck with it."

That was my first indication that I had a chance. I had to go to a meeting in Scottsdale, Arizona, with the Labor Relations Board. My wife was going with me. I told her to call the foundation and tell them we would like to meet with them about the house we were thinking of building on the island. When I got home, I asked her what the foundation said. She told me they couldn't meet with me because there was not enough time. When we were getting ready to leave for the trip, I rolled up the drawings I had created and put them in my suitcase. My wife asked why I was taking them. I said, "Because I'm going to meet with The Frank Lloyd Wright Foundation." When we got to Scottsdale, I went directly to Taliesin West. I walked into the store, and they asked me if I would like to have a tour of Taliesin. I said, "No, thank you, I'm here to meet an architect to go over building a house that Frank Lloyd Wright designed," and I rolled out my drawing. She made a phone call, and in a few minutes, an architect showed up. I showed him the drawings. He asked where we were planning on building it.

I said, "On the island that it was designed for, in New York."

"Aren't you worried about blocking your neighbors view?"

"I don't have any neighbors, it's on a private island and I own it."

Five minutes later, there were four architects talking with us. I guess a week in advance was too short of notice for just anybody, but when you own your own private island that FLW designed a home for, time was no longer an issue. They had a program for building Frank Lloyd Wright houses using the plans they had in the archives. For five percent of the cost of construction, they would design the house for you. For ten percent of the construction costs, they would design a house for you and allow you to say that it was "inspired by" Frank Lloyd Wright. For fifteen percent of the construction costs, they would design the house for you and allow you to call it an "authentic" Frank Lloyd Wright house.

I called Tom Heinz and told him about my meeting with the foundation. He had heard about the program they offered. I told Tom that I wanted the foundation to do the drawings so the house could be an authentic FLW masterpiece. He said he understood. The next thing I wanted was for the foundation to make a rendering of the house in color, so I could show it to the town when I applied for my permits. We went back and forth on the price for the rendering and settled on 5000 dollars, which would come off my fee for the drawings the foundation would provide. The renderings came out beautiful; they were breathtaking. The next job I had was to hire a lawyer to put everything together and hopefully get the town to issue a building permit. I didn't have a lot of hope that the town would let me build it.

They had a 100-foot setback for anything built on the lake, and the house cantilevered over the water by 30 feet. That meant I needed a 130-foot setback variance; I didn't think my chances were very good. I hired a local lawyer, William A. Shilling, who was familiar with the town and the planning board. We met to come up with a plan to present to town. Petra Island was broken up into three building lots. We proposed to make it one building lot.

There were four buildings on Petra Island. The Frank Lloyd Wright cottage, a caretaker's cottage, a small building right on the water, and a two-story house on the opposite side of the island. We proposed eliminating the caretaker's cottage and making it a workshop, along with abandoning the two-story house on the opposite side of the island. That would reduce the number of bedrooms by four, and that was how many bedrooms the new house would have. That would be everything we needed to present to the planning board.

I had been working with the Frank Lloyd Wright Foundation, trying to get them to commit to a price to make the working drawings on the project. You would think they would be very interested in the project; there had not been a Frank Lloyd Wright house built on the property it was designed for in over 60 years. The project, building Frank's masterpiece, would put the foundation back on the map. After going back and forth with the foundation, I finally got a call from the fellow I was working with, and he said to me, "Joe, I have a number for you." I knew it wouldn't be cheap; I was expecting a number in the hundred thousand dollar range. He said to me, "You need to sit down before I give you the number, they're crazy. They want 450,000 dollars to do the drawings." I didn't even believe him. I told him to stop joking and give me the real number, but he said it was the real number. He then added whatever detail *they* put on the drawing, which I had to include in the building. I said to him,

"Whose house is this? Theirs or mine? Can't you talk some sense into them?"

"I already tried, they weren't budging. One other thing you're not going to be happy with," he added, "They said if you don't use them, you can't build the house because they own the copyright."

"I'll have to think about all of this and will get back to you."

All he could say was that he was sorry.

If the house was built on the mainland and not on an island, I estimated the house could be built for 350 dollars per square foot. If you did the math using the square foot price, the house would cost 1,700,000 dollars to build. Investing the 15% that the foundation wanted to produce the drawings and stamp it as a Frank Lloyd Wright house would come up to 200,000 dollars. Because the house was going to be built on an island, the construction costs went up. That should not change the price it would cost to do the drawings.

I kicked this around for a while. I figured that it would cost me at least a hundred thousand dollars to get somebody to do the drawings and then another hundred thousand dollars to fight the foundation in court for the copyright. I went back to them and offered two hundred thousand dollars. In the meantime, we had a date set to meet with the planning department to get a building permit. The foundation turned me down and wouldn't move off the 450,000 number to do the drawings. I told them I would have somebody else do the drawings and thanked them for their service. The day before the town meeting, the foundation sent a letter to the town asking them not to approve the building of the house because they owned the copyright on the drawings. The town notified us about this. *Well, I guess that's the end of this project... Right!* I sat down with my lawyer, and what we decided was to tell the town that we would hold them not liable for it.

I never expected this project to be easy; as a matter of fact, I never expected to ever be approved by the town. There was a 44-acre island on the lake that the town would never let anybody build on. But that didn't mean I wasn't going to try; you must know my method by now. "No" meant "go," and I just kept going. My first goal was to figure out a way to beat them at their copyright game. A few years back, I lost a patent infringement case with Construction Technology. I got to know the lawyers pretty well during that battle, and the first thing I thought was if they were good enough to kick my butt, maybe they could help me fight this copyright issue. I called them to talk to them about the copyright problem I was having. They told me they could not handle the case due to a conflict of interest with the company that sued me — plan B.

One day, I was on the island with a friend of mine named Ed Barnet, his wife and daughter, and his daughter's boyfriend, who happened to be a copyright lawyer in the music industry. Now, you all know how lucky I had always been. His hobby just happened to be architectural copyright law. We started talking about the problem with the foundation, and the lawyer said to me, "We can beat them!" I used my extraordinary patience while making a big decision and hired him on the spot. What we did was sue them for all their copyrights. Our point was they didn't have much to lose if we just sued them for my copyright, but if they had to worry about all their copyrights, that might change things. We filed a lawsuit.

I called Tom Heinz and said to him, "Remember when I told you that you had no chance to be the architect of record on this

257

project? Well, you can't always believe what you hear, or what I say." After long deliberation, about three minutes, I hired him to be the architect on the project. When you need to go in front of the planning board for a public hearing on your project, you want to try to pick a night when a lot of people are not going to attend the meeting. The fewer the people, the better the chances. When my lawyer and I walked into that meeting, over 100 people were sitting there. My lawyer looked at me and said, "This is not good, Joe." We sat down and waited for our turn to present in front of the Board. It didn't take too long before we realized that all the people were at the meeting for another problem, not our permit. Who's the luckiest guy you know? Me.

The president of the Planning Board was a member of my golf club and a friend of mine. When it was our turn, we had the two renderings sitting on an easel in front of the room. They were covered over so that nobody could see. When my lawyer started the presentation, I lifted the cover to the first rendering, showing the house's floor plan. Then, I flipped to the other rendering, which was the side view showing the house hanging over the lake. All you could hear was 100 people taking a deep breath. The renderings were absolutely magnificent. After the presentation by my lawyer, the Planning Board president opened the meeting up for public comment. That was where the critical part began. He waited about two minutes… nobody raised their hand. He closed the public comment portion of the meeting and advised us that the Board would get back to us with any other questions they had. Before the meeting, there were concerns from the Fire Department and Police Department. They didn't want to be liable for something happening out there, so we would have to sign a waiver that they did not have to provide their services as part of the deal. It was another step forward for having a chance to build the magnificent house.

The Frank Loyd Wright Foundation applied to the courts for a change of venue. They wanted to move the trial from New York to Arizona. The judge asked them where the house was being built.

They said, "New York," so the judge said, "The case stays here."

My lawyer called me and said, "Joe, they want to talk to you one more time to see if they can resolve this before court. Don't settle for more than 50,000 dollars. It will cost us no more than 50,000 dollars to win this case." They had a new president who wanted to talk to me. I called him up and told him exactly what had happened where I had offered them 200,000 dollars.

"They turned me down, and they sent a notice to the town telling them they had a copyright on the house and I could not build the house."

He said to me, "My people were pretty stupid. How do we resolve this?"

I said, "Very very simple, you leave me alone and I leave you alone."

He agreed with the deal, but he wanted us not to call it an original Frank Lloyd Wright house. Instead, he wanted me to say that the house was inspired by Frank Lloyd Wright. I didn't have a problem with that because Frank inspired me to build his masterpiece just like he wanted. Then it would be a Frank Lloyd Wright original. I called my lawyer back and told him to settle the case. He asked what it cost me to settle, so I told him, "Nothing."

"How did you do that?"

"That's what I do."

I was still having a hard time with my forced retirement. The restaurant did not take that much of my time, and neither had the house project so far. With the computer company in Boston, my role was that of a consultant only. That could've all changed the day they would issue me a building permit.

CHAPTER XXVII

Building My Team

It started to look like my retirement was over. Things were moving forward with the house project. The first big test came when we needed a perk test. A perk test is used to determine how much water the dirt can retain, which would tell us if we could put a working septic system in place. What I was worried about was that the island was nothing but a big rock that the glacier could not move; I was pretty sure that rock didn't hold much water. I hired an engineer to perform the test and directed him to perform it where the cottage's existing septic field was. I thought that might be the safest place, and sure enough, it was. The perk test came out perfect.

The next thing I knew, the impossible happened. The town issued me a building permit on April 16, 2003. *What's wrong with these people? Now I'm going to have to build this project.* It was a good thing I didn't realize how big this project was at the time. Just like all the other projects that were too big for me, I just kept moving forward. Tom had been working on the drawings the best he could. The problem with these small-scale drawings was that there were some details we hadn't been able to figure out. I was contacted by one of the sons of the original owner. He happened to live in the next town over. He had heard about the project and wanted to meet me. I set up a meeting with him when Tom Heinz was in town. We met on the island which he grew up on. It had been years since he was last on the island; you could see his emotions.

***

Meet Dodd Chahroudi. We talked about the main house that was never built, and I showed him the drawings we had. He told us he had copies of the original full-size drawings. I looked at Tom, Tom looked at me, and we knew right then that everything was going to fall into the *Wright* place. We drove together over to his apartment. He had the drawings rolled up in a closet. Sure enough, he unrolled the copies of the original Frank Lloyd Wright drawings. It was like a piece of artwork. Suddenly, we could see the details that were missing from the small drawings. We asked him if we could make copies of these for our use. He agreed. *Who's the luckiest guy?* He also had a videotape of his father explaining his meeting with Frank Lloyd Wright and discussing the house; he gave us a copy of it as well. The meeting with Dodd was exactly what we needed to propel the project to the next step.

The next thing I needed to do was to hire a structural engineer. There was a member of my club who worked for a large structural engineering company. At the time, his company was working on a structural problem on Frank Lloyd Wright's famous Fallingwater home. Apparently, the cantilever on that house was falling down. It was only half the size of the cantilever we were proposing to build on our house. I met with him to go over our project and hired him to produce the structural drawings for 15,000 dollars. Tom and I started working on the bidding package to detail the work that we needed done on the island. I wanted to break it into two phases: phase one would be constructing the building itself without the interior work, and phase two would be the interior work, including all the woodwork, cabinets, ceilings, and walls.

My country club had a beach on the lake right across from my island. My original plan called for me to rent the beach to stage my work from. I proposed to put in a concrete dock at the beach where I could load the barges with material and transport that material to the island. After the project was complete, the golf course would be able to use the dock to rent space for boats. I would have another barge docked at the island with the crane and a concrete pump on it to pump the concrete up to the house. I found a company that could provide the barges for the job. That type of barge would be assembled when they were in the water. I went back to my golf club and gave them a proposal. Then I went over everything with them. They got back to me within a week with approval on everything I wanted to do. The club president was my golf partner and friend Andrew Young; I think being friends with the president had some perks.

The next thing I had to do was submit the plans to the EPA since I was working in the lake to build the dock I was proposing. While I waited for an answer from EPA, we continued working on the bidding documentation. I was waiting on the structural drawings to be able to go out to bid. All I needed was a preliminary drawing to estimate from. Every time I ran into the structural engineer at the club, I would bug for my drawings. One day, he called me and said, "Let's meet. I have a preliminary drawing." We met at the club, he rolled out the drawing, and I couldn't believe my eyes. I said,

"What did you do here? You have the roof framed in wood and you have a 60-foot steel beam as part of the roof. This roof has to be concrete like everything else; this is not what was in the original drawings I gave you."

He said, "You can't build the house with concrete."

"It was designed in concrete. Looking at the original drawings, each wall was placed in a position to support that roof. Anybody that has been in the construction business knows that it's a concrete roof. Do not go any further on these drawings."

I called my architect Tom and told him what I just saw. He said, "You have to be kidding me. Let me make a few calls to see if I can find the right structural engineer."

I sent the first structural engineer a letter demanding my money back. He said that he was not going to give the money back. A week later, I sent him a bill for 100,000 dollars and a letter that said, "15,000 dollars for the money you owe me, and 85,000 because of the delay you caused on this project." A week later, I received my $15,000 back.

The new structural engineer was out of New Mexico, and his name was Auggie. His specialty was post-tension concrete decks. He took one look at their original drawings and knew it was a 6-inch thick reinforced concrete roof. I had one request for Auggie, and that was to add an extra one inch of concrete where I planned to put the helicopter landing pad on the roof. Our bid documents were finally complete. I wanted a midsize company that was very familiar with concrete work; the house was built out of concrete, stone, and mahogany. I started my bidders list with a few contractors I already knew. A few other contractors had heard about the project and sent me letters stating they would like to bid on it, so I added them to the list. We went out to bid to six contractors in early September of 2003. We received the bids back in a couple of weeks. It was kind of what I expected; most of them were scared to death of the project. The prices were all over the place. I had prepared my own estimate of the project with a ballpark number I was looking for. Most of the bids were way over my estimate. There was one bid that was near my estimate. Tom &

I were worried that he could not handle the project. I was not comfortable at all with any of them.

Most weekends, I was playing golf at the club with Richard, Greg, and Andrew. My foursome had the early tee time. So every Saturday morning, at 7 a.m. on my ride to the club, I would pass by this beautiful house that was under construction. I saw a woman telling the workers what to do. She had these guys hustling by seven a.m. every Saturday. I still had not decided on the contractor who would be building my house. One morning, I got a call from my friend Charlie over at the marina. He was wondering if I had found a contractor for the job yet. I told him I had a few bids, but nobody I was really excited about. He asked if I knew the woman who was building houses around the lake. Her name was Lidia. As it turned out, she was the woman I kept seeing on my ride to the club every Saturday morning. Charlie called to tell me that Lidia was the one who I wanted to build on my house. I took a set of my drawings and my specifications over to the job site where she was working.

When she looked at the plans of the house, her mouth dropped open. She said she would be definitely interested and would put some numbers together for me. She called me the next day and asked if we could get together and go over our numbers. We got together that afternoon and started talking about the project. She knew more about the project in a short amount of time since she had seen the drawings compared to any of the other contractors that bid on the job. She took out three yellow sheets of paper with the estimate handwritten on them. I took out my three sheets of white paper that I had handwritten my own estimate, and we started comparing notes. Her estimates came close to my original number. I thought we both knew that the number we came up with was really competitive. To do the job under contract price and make sure that you survived at the end of it, you would have to double the number that we both had. The only possible way to finish the project would be on "time and material" with that as our target number. I liked her right away. She was a "get-it-done" person. I used my long-standing decision-making method, and on November 3, 2003, I hired Lydia on the spot.

***

Meet Lidia Wusatowska; she was trained in Poland as an aeronautical engineer. She came to America and became a general contractor. Her core working crew was also from Poland and were well skilled in every trade. Each one of her men could perform any task. One day a plumber, the next day a carpenter, and the next day a mason. I assembled a core team for this project with Tom Heinz as the architect, Augie Mosiman as the structural engineer, Lidia Wusatowska as the general contractor, Barbara Massaro as the interior designer, and Joe Massaro, recently out of retirement, as the construction manager.

CHAPTER XXVIII
Getting Started Wright

We had our first team meeting together in the cottage on the island. I wanted to start construction in early March when the ice was off the lake. That would give us four months for our pre-planning. Time was not something I was used to having on big projects. I just received the answer from the DEC on the dock at the golf course. They rejected it. At the meeting, I told them about the rejection and said that I would spend the next couple of months trying to get the permit. Lydia said to me,

"Joe, we don't need that dock. I can build the house without it."

I asked, "Where do we launch the barges from if we didn't have the dock?"

"We don't need barges, just a couple of pontoon boats."

The three of us planned a trip to visit Frank Lloyd Wright's house built around the same time he designed this one. Between that house and the cottage, we should've had enough details to finish our drawings. If not, we could go to Tom's Library to compare different details from other Wright houses in the same time span. I told him I wanted to build this Frank Lloyd Wright's house as though Frank was standing beside me. According to the book "The Many Faces of Frank Lloyd Wright," this was Frank's favorite design. My goal was to build the house so close to the original drawings that if Frank walked through the door and looked at his masterpiece, it would take his breath away.

That would make me satisfied.

The house we were going to visit was in a neighborhood called Usonia in Westchester County, New York. The idea was to get a lot of detailed ideas from that house. It was built around the same time Frank designed my house. The house was owned by Roland Reiscey. There were several Wright homes in that specific community. We thanked Mr. Reiscey for inviting us, and he said we could come back anytime if we needed more information. The three of us met for the next three days in the cottage. Each one of us had a task to do. We had open lines of communication; if one of us needed information from the other person, we just called. Tom would be doing most of his work from Chicago. Our job was to line up the other contractors like electricians and plumbers and start working on the long lead items we needed. For instance, the plans called for 26 skylights to be custom-built; they would take a while.

We set up telephone conference meetings at least twice a week. I forgot how good it felt! I knew that I would be running at that pace for at least the next three years. There were going to be hurdles along the way. Nothing I hadn't already jumped, "I think."

We worked on the list of equipment we needed to build the job, like an excavator, small truck, and concrete mixers. *How are we going to get them out there?* I needed to look at the barges again.

It was time for me to head to Florida and for Tom to get back to Chicago. We kept in touch and kept working on our tasks. Timing of material was critical to keep a job on schedule. In the sheet metal business, if your timing was off, you could go back into the job site after a day, and all the walls would be in your way. Now, instead of working off a rolling scaffold, you would have to work with individual ladders. So I was a stickler about getting the scheduling right.

In late January, I was in Florida working on obtaining different types of material for the project. I knew that they had a cold winter up there in New York. I remembered that years ago, people used to race cars on Lake Mahopac in the winter. I started doing some research on how much weight the ice could hold. It turned out that ice was pretty strong. Twelve inches of ice could hold 11,000 pounds. That would be enough ice to get a lot of material over to the island. I called my friend Charlie at the Marina. It was a cold January day there, so I asked him if he would go over to the country club and measure ice thickness from there to my island. He thought I was crazy, but I didn't explain myself. I said, "I'll tell you what I'm doing next week, just go out and get me some measurements, you need the exercise."

The next day, he called me to tell me the ice's average thickness was over 30 inches. My chart said 30 inches of ice would hold 70 tons. I would be able to build the house on the mainland and move it there! I called Lydia, and when she answered the phone, I said,

"Are you ready to go to work?"

"The lake is frozen solid."

"I know, it's the perfect time to go to work." I explained to her what I learned about the strength of ice. I explained my new plan that included moving the excavator over and everything else she needed before the ice got any thinner. By my estimates, we had about four weeks to move equipment. I told her to stage everything on the beach at the golf course, and I would be back in a week.

When I got back from Florida, the beach looked like a construction site. It had equipment and material all over. Lidia was ready to go, but I noticed one problem: she was planning to use snowmobiles to pull the stuff across the ice about a half-mile. I told her they were not going to work because they wouldn't have enough traction. She didn't believe me, so she tried them anyway. Sure enough, she pulled the first load, and the snowmobile just threw the snow out of the back end. I told her we needed a six-wheel gator. The next morning, she had two gators ready to go. She was pretty amazing! They hooked the first gator up to a pile of wood and started going across the ice and snow. It had no problem pulling that stuff across the ice, right up onto the island. We started full swing, gators going back and forth being loaded at the beach and unloaded on the island. She bought brand-new oil tanks, cut them in half, and filled them with gravel. Then, she pulled them across the ice. It was beautiful to watch.

In the beginning, the men driving the equipment were worried about the thickness of the ice. After two trips, they were confident. However, the real test was the excavator; it weighed 15,000 pounds. Thank God nobody from the town was around when we started moving the excavator. They had the driver of the excavator wear a life jacket with a rope tied around his waist, just in case... Two men walked alongside the excavator in case it went through the ice. If that happened, the men walking could pull the driver to safety. Everybody was nervous as that excavator crept along. I was most worried when we were in the middle, between the island and the beach. Just before we reached the island, the tracks broke through, water came out, and everybody froze!

Luckily, we were only in six inches of water. The excavator drove up onto the beach, and everybody clapped. The driver of the excavator said something in Polish. When I asked Lydia what he said, she said, "He's not driving it back!" Everybody laughed. We worked seven days a week through February. It was amazing how much material we moved. We ended up with one excavator, one backhoe, two six-wheel gators, six cement mixers, hundreds of bags of concrete, piles of sand and gravel, reinforcing bars, and thousands of feet of wood for framing. It was a very successful operation. Now was time to get off the ice.

We spent the next few weeks planning the job while we waited for the ice to break apart so we can get back out to the island and start working. In late March, we were able to start. The first thing we did was clear the trees from where the house was going to be built. I was in Florida when Lydia called me to ask what she should do with the trees that she cut down. I told her to burn them. Two days later, she called me and told me that the town had fined her for an open fire. I asked her how much they fined her, and she said 500 dollars. I said, "That is less than it would have cost to move the wood off the island." By early April, I flew back to New York, ready to work.

CHAPTER XXIX
Starting Phase I

When I got back to New York, I met with Lydia and Tom on the island to lay out the house's location. All the trees and the stumps were removed from the area, and we had also excavated down to the rock. Mr. Wright designed his prairie houses on a grid. He would lay down lines on a piece of paper five feet apart in one direction and five feet apart in another direction at a 30° angle. It would be a complete grid system. It was the same system he used on the cottage, except they were three feet apart. Then he would lay out the walls on the grid. If we could match the grid's starting line to the island, then we would place the house exactly where he wanted it. In Wright's drawing, he gave us the exact start of the first grid line; it was amazing. The large rock that the house was designed around had an obvious notch in it. That notch was shown on his drawing, and it was where the first line of his grid started. I never thought math was important in school, but man, was it important in life!

The first job Lydia wanted to tackle was the 75-foot living room cantilever. That one area took over 50% of the concrete that we would use on the entire job. It was the most difficult part of the job. The first part of that was building the octagonal column at the edge of the island, which would support that slab. We had to excavate down to bedrock. The bedrock was slanted, so we had to remove rock to make sure that it was flat on the bottom; otherwise, the column could walk itself down the hill, bringing the entire cantilever with it. Once we flattened out the rock, we drilled holes and placed epoxy and rebar into every hole.

The column was 10 feet in diameter and 20 feet high. It was going to be poured solid because it would be holding up to 300,000 pounds of concrete. Once it was poured and set, we started framing out for the concrete slab. The slab was going to be 2-feet thick with two layers of rebar and post-tensioning cabling every 2 feet in both directions. The wood framing for the slab was going to be reinforced with two by sixes back to back every 12 inches. The framing was needed to support all that weight before the concrete would set.

Once the framing was done, then we would lay out the post-tension cables. After completing the layout, Auggie, the engineer, came onto the job site and informed me that we laid them out incorrectly. He said we had to move everyone up by one inch! That was how critical the post-tension cables were. We had already drilled hundreds of holes and set receptacles for every cable. The cables were 5/8 of an inch thick with a plastic sheathing over it. Once they were laid in the correct place, we were ready to pour the slab. I asked Lydia when we were going to pour the slab. She was working on getting the exact concrete mix. The engineer needed 8000 PSI. We were planning to mix the concrete by hand, which would've been very difficult to maintain the exact consistency.

Another week went by, and she made several mixes and had them tested. She told me she was still not happy with the exact formula. Finally, she found the perfect mix, and we were ready to start pouring. She came up with an ingenious plan to maintain the concrete mix's consistency while we mixed it by hand. She mixed the exact ingredients in different colored buckets. All the laborers had to do was mix two red buckets, a green bucket, and a half of a yellow bucket with the exact amount of water; the mix would be the same no matter who mixed it. It was going to be what they called a monolithic pour. You could not stop during the process; the entire slab had to be poured in one continuous time. If you had to stop because of electrical power failure, the entire slab would be no good.

The other thing we worried about was whether we had enough supports underneath the slab. We had no engineering on the supports. You could not walk through the supports because there were too many. We had 20 men on each shift to help with the concrete. We mixed and poured concrete for 36 hours nonstop. When the concrete pump got clogged, we would use wheelbarrows to continue moving concrete. Tom suggested that we put the concrete pump up higher than the floor; in case there was a jam.

The weight pushing on the flow would prevent jams. The more the concrete was poured, the more creaking you could hear coming from the wood supports. Lydia wasn't worried; she said it was good noise and that it was creaking right. It was a long night, but when the morning came and the forms held, we all finally breathed. We tested the concrete, and it was better than the engineer wanted; it was 10,000 p.s.i.

The next area we started working on was the entrance and the 20-foot high support for the master bedroom. It was the only point of the building that entered the water. We had a wetlands permit that allowed us to build up to the water's edge. It took several months to get all of the permits I needed to build the house. When I wanted to build the dock at the golf course, the Department of Environmental Conservation (D.E.C.) turned me down because they didn't want concrete in the water. The part we were about to build had a small footprint in the water. I decided not to seek permission for that section. I believed my wetlands permit would cover it. I received a call from a friend of mine telling me he saw somebody at the shore with binoculars watching the construction. I didn't think very much of it; after all, it was a very interesting project.

One Sunday, the doorbell rang at my shore house. I opened the door to find a guy in uniform wearing a gun. He handed me a piece of paper and said I was in violation, and I was handed a stop-work order. He said I was building in the lake without a permit. I told him I had all of my permits in place, but he told me to take it up in court. According to the paperwork, there were three areas in violation. One was the area at the bottom of the steps that we were currently working on, another area was the construction road we put along the lake, and the third area was the wood we had in the lake holding up the cantilever.

On Monday morning, I informed Lydia about the problem and told her to stop working in those areas. She asked me what we were going to do. I told her we had to get it straightened out some way. I didn't know how yet, but the one thing I did know was we were not going to stop the project; it would be completed one way or another. We had plenty of other areas to work on until I took care of the problem. I knew the marina in town worked with the DEC getting their boat docks in place. I called my friend Charlie and asked him if he knew anybody at the DEC. I told him about my problem, and he said he knew the boss there. He told me he would call him and see what could be done.

Charlie called me back a few days later. He told me he got in touch with the head of the D.E.C., and he would come out in a couple of weeks. I needed to do some pre-planning before the meeting. My theory was going to be that when the lake was at its lowest level, the area I was working in was above the water and my wetlands permit covered it. Within a couple of weeks, I would be able to take all the forms away that were holding up the cantilever out of the water. That would take care of that violation. As far as the road was concerned, I could show that I did not change the shoreline; I only reinforced the construction road. My biggest problem was the 20-foot tall wall with its foundation in the water. I made a drawing showing the high and low water levels in the lake, and where the foundation was in relation to the low water level.

Two weeks later, Charlie called me and said the DEC was coming out to discuss the problem. The next day, as I was standing on the cantilever. I saw a boat approaching with Charlie, the officer who served me, and the head of the D.E.C. As they pulled up near the cantilever, the head of D.E.C looked up and waved to me, and he asked how I was doing. I knew right then that I could negotiate with that guy. They pulled up to the old dock and tied the boat up. I noticed that the head of the D.E.C. had a bad leg. I said to him, "We don't have to go up there. I can show you right here why I don't need a permit from you." I took out my drawings and started showing him the reason why I didn't need a permit. He told me to stop. He said, "We both know you're BSing me but the good news is, it's not as bad as I thought it would be." He told me to file for a permit, and he would grant it, but I would still have to go to court over the violation.

A couple of days later, I went to court. The judge says to the enforcement officer, "I understand you guys settled, what is the fine?" Knowing the DEC, the fine could've been huge. The officer said, "500 dollars." I never wrote a check so fast in my life. Going back to that old philosophy that I often live by, it's better to ask forgiveness than seek permission. The head of D.E.C. told me that I probably would've gotten it if I had filed for the permit earlier. We cleared another hurdle, and we were back on track, ready to go to work.

Whenever we could, we built a model and tested different building methods. For instance, the walls of the house, unlike the cottage, had to be insulated. We had to pass the N.Y. State energy code. We passed by only 1%, and all of them needed to be bearing walls. They had built a 2-foot high form on the cottage, where they put rocks into and poured concrete into it. They continued that method until the wall was completely poured. We knew we couldn't use this method. We built a sample wall with the new product. It was a 4 x 8 sheet of 4-inch Styrofoam, with metal mesh on each side. We would slide the rebar between the metal mesh in the Styrofoam and put 4-inch concrete on each side of the wall.

We finally had our insulated structural wall. We needed to develop a method to incorporate the rocks with the wall to look similar to the cottage walls. What we came up with was to drill two holes in the back of each rock along with two holes that matched into the concrete wall. We used the exact same hole pattern on every rock; that way, we could move rocks around until we were satisfied with the pattern. We took a piece of rebar and used it to attach the rock to the wall. After we were satisfied with the positioning of the rocks, we covered the face of the rocks with laundry detergent and sprayed on an additional 2 inches of concrete. The laundry detergent stopped the concrete from sticking to the rock's face. We used this method for all the walls we built on the project. I didn't know how we could've built the project without the Internet. I had products coming from all over the country. The skylights were 8-foot triangles. The only place that had an oven almost big enough to build them was in California. I had to cut down the size of the skylight by half of an inch to fit in the oven. We had 26 dome-shaped insulated skylights in this house.

I designed the heating and air-conditioning system over the winter. It was going to be six zones so I could hide all the ductwork. I needed 10 tons of air conditioning just for the skylight area. I had to buy all of the ductwork from my competitor because I sold my sheet metal business. Luckily, a couple of my best friends owned ABM Heating and Air Conditioning. Remember them from Mike's pizza shop? Richard and Greg did all the work at Mike's, and now they were going to take care of my island. It helps to have friends!

***

Greg had a great friend who was in the woodworking business. He had a shop in Norwalk, Connecticut, and could build all of the custom interior wood that we needed out of African Mahogany. Meet Fred Wilmont. I met him on a golf trip. Greg, the pilot, would fly us to different parts of the south every spring and fall to play golf. Fred was in business with his two sons. I took all three of them to different Frank Lloyd Wright houses to show them what the details would look like for our windows, doors, cabinetry, and interior wood. Everything we needed, I had Fred make a sample of. Every piece he created came out perfect.

The next item we needed to figure out was the copper fascia that went around the entire house. I did not have a friend in the copper industry, so I had to dig for it. The copper fascia in the front of the house was 4 feet high, and in the back of the house, 2-feet high. Each panel was 4 feet wide and had a geometrical pattern. I built a male and a female die of the pattern out of wood. I then put a copper panel in between the male and the female and drove my truck over it to try and create the pattern on the copper panel. It didn't come out very good, but you could see the image enough to get an idea of what it would look like. I then took the wooden die, put a new piece of copper in it, and took it to my friend's machine shop who had a large press. We put the die in the press and stepped on the petal. When I heard the press break hit the die, I said, "Boy that's going to do it." It definitely had the image on it when we took it apart, but all the corners were crinkled. That was not going to work either. I had to make hundreds of these panels, and they could not have crinkly edges.

***

I was at the annual Heating and Air Conditioning show with my son-in-law a few weeks later. Meet David; my younger daughter Jennifer married him shortly after she finished college. He was an engineering student who came to work at East Coast Sheet Metal after they were married. He was a sharp kid, and I was happy to teach him the industry. We had a booth at the show displaying our software products. I knew there was a company that made custom air outlets for air conditioning there. I wanted something special for my island's Frank Loyd Wright house. I went over to their booth and started talking to a young man about my air outlets. It just so happened that he owned a Frank Lloyd Wright House on Long Island. What were the chances of that? *Who's the luckiest guy around?*

I showed him the plans of my house, and we talked about the air outlets that he said he could build. I had details of the copper panels I needed, so I showed them to him and asked if he knew anybody who could fabricate the panels. He looked at it and said he could do it himself. When I got back from the show, I sent him a computer program of the patterns I needed. He called me a few days later and told me to come down to his shop to show me what he created. The shop was in Brooklyn. I took a ride down, and sure enough, he had a copper panel with exactly what I wanted. I gave him the job.

The next area we started working on was the back end of the house. In that area, we needed to remove about two feet of rock. I didn't want to use dynamite because it would shake up the whole town. I was trying to keep a low profile out here. Even my cement mixers were electric instead of gas to keep the construction noise down. I found a product out of Germany that cracked the rock with a simple white clay powder, some water, and a hole only an inch deep. The only problem with that method was that the rock was so hard that we had to use a lot of drill bits. We ended up buying every 1-inch drill bit we could find in the two surrounding counties.

We set up a woodworking shop in the cottage to build the wooden forms needed to frame out the skylight area. It was very detailed work. We were using furniture-grade plywood for the forms so that when we removed the forms, the concrete faces would be perfectly smooth. My workers had been living on the island since we started the project. We were getting ready to shut down for the rest of winter. A lot of these workers would go back to Poland for holidays. We would be ready to continue the project once the ice melted in the spring of the following year. Everything was going well so far. We had a great team: Lydia, her workers, and Tom Heinz, the architect. I was excited to continue next year, but I was ready to go to Florida and get a little R & R.

In February, I received a report from my marina that the ice was not strong that year, so we couldn't move anything over. Everything would be moved by pontoon boats instead. Good thing we got the concrete poured when the ice was thick!

CHAPTER XXX
Year II Building Wright

The original drawings never contained any interior details, but plenty of drawings were available for us to build the shell of the house. We could see the built-in furniture and the kitchen cabinets in these drawings, but no examples of useful living furniture. All of the windows and doors were shown in FLW's drawings, but none of the finer details. For this information, Tom Heinz was our go-to expert. He studied and took pictures of most of Frank Lloyd Wright's houses. He'd written several books and had Frank Lloyd Wright's furniture built. Between Tom and I, we had a complete library of books dedicated to Mr. Wright's work. If there was a detail that we needed, we would go through the books and look at houses he designed and built during the same time. For instance, in the master bedroom, I wanted a different rock pattern on the walls and the fireplace in that room. In one of the books, I found the details of rock work done at Fallingwater; that's what I chose. I wanted a different rock pattern for the fireplace in the library. Again, I looked at another book and picked out a pattern that Frank had used in one of his houses. Of course, I would discuss these selections with Tom and Lydia. If Tom did not agree with me, I would tell him, "I have to do it that way… Frank came to me last night in a dream and told me to do it like that."

I would be on the job site every day. If problems came up, I would call Tom and discuss the problem with him. If we couldn't fix a problem over the phone, Tom would fly up from Chicago. By mid-summer, phase one of the construction project would be completed. My original plan was to go out to bid for phase two for all the finished work. Lydia had done such a good job and had such a good team already in place; we decided to keep her on board for phase two. While we were finishing the concrete work, Fred Wilmont was building the doors and windows. We had two pontoon boats moving everything from the mainland to the island. We had been ahead of the curve, getting all the material to the job site in a timely manner. It was time to start installing the heating and air conditioning ductwork. Richard and Gregory from ABM had completed the fabrication, and we had everything on the job site ready to start.

I was planning on installing it all myself. It felt like I was going back in time, working on a scaffold installing ductwork, if only Pete was there to yell at me. If something was too heavy for me, the workers on the job would give me a hand. When the entranceway was stripped of the construction forms, and the skylights were set in place, it became an amazing sight to see. It was one of the moments that reminded me why we went ahead with the project. Frank Lloyd Wright had a vision, and when the skylight forms came down, I could suddenly see his vision clear as day.

I was still toying with the copper panels and which pattern to use, as there was no detail in the drawings. I found a company that made thick Styrofoam panels. They routed out the geometric designs in and then infused them with liquid copper. I had one of the panels from my contractor in Brooklyn ship it to me, and I installed both of them next to each other as a sample. The Styrofoam panel had a 1-inch depression for the geometric pattern. The copper panel had a small raised geometrical pattern on it. I left them there for Tom, Lydia, Barbara, and I to look at for a while before making a final decision. The Styrofoam panels stood right out, being that the design called for so many of them; I felt like they would be all you saw when you first looked at the house. The copper panels were much more subtle. Depending on which way the sun was facing, the geometrical forms would change. We all chose the copper panels. Copper expands and contracts more than any other metal. I came up with a slip method where we could put the panels together, making them waterproof, and the panels could move without buckling. My old shop built the connecting slip and all the corners that were used on the fascia.

When all the copper panels were completed and shipped to the job site, I had the workers put them on the roof for me. I laid each panel on the roof where it was to be installed and then started installing every panel myself. They came out great; I am still waiting for them to turn green. I might not be here to see when they completely turn green, but it will definitely change the house's entire image.

The next big job was to install the African Mahogany panels on the ceilings. Those were eight-inch wide tongue and groove boards. The V- notch was a special angle that only Frank Lloyd Wright used. Freddy, my woodworker, had to have special dies made to produce the tongue and groove. When we installed the concrete roof, we used the same material that we built the walls with; 4 inches thick Styrofoam with wire mesh on each side. We poured four inches of concrete on the outside except where I planned to put the helicopter pad. There, we poured six inches of concrete there.

On the inside, we left the wire mesh exposed so we could slide wood strips in between the mesh to use to fasten the ceiling to. I wanted all the woodwork installed with what they called blind nailing. No nails would be seen in the face of the wood. The ceiling heights from the entrance way to the living room were 12 feet high. That was unheard of in a Frank Lloyd Wright house since most of his designs contained very low ceilings. There was only one square corner in the entire house. Most of the walls had a 10-degree angle. For most of my life, I estimated jobs and was pretty good at it by now. Estimating how much wood we would need for the house would prove to be more challenging than any job I estimated in my 30-year career! I placed the first order, and we started installing. By the time we finished the house, I had placed five orders for wood. There was so much waste because of all the angles; it was unbelievable. Good thing I wasn't getting paid for this estimating job!

Most of the lighting in the house was indirect lighting. Each room had a soffit inside with lights sitting on top of the soffit. We used the low-voltage Lutron system for lighting. In each room, lighting was made up of two components. The first one was a low voltage light on a sort of dimmer to control the brightness. If that was not enough light, the second component was a fluorescent light that brightened everything up. Everything in the house was electric, including the heat. There was electric radiant heat on every floor, and the air conditioners were also heat pumps with the backup electric coil if the temperature went below 40 degrees. We had 800 amps coming into the house.

We had a high-voltage line coming under the lake to a transformer near the house. The underwater cable was already there when I purchased the island. When Mr.Chahroudi went out to Arizona to meet with Frank Lloyd Wright and go over the drawings, Frank pointed out what some details represented. For instance, Frank told him the windows overlooking the lake were like musical notes. You could see it when you looked at them. He also told him that the geometrical designs on the copper panels represented the waves on the lake.

There were three bedrooms in the back of the house, and the master bedroom was completely separated from them. Frank said the master bedroom was to be an island within an island. We were so lucky to have these intimate details. They felt like a gift from Frank, so we could build his masterpiece the way he saw it. I truly believed it was Frank's favorite house he had ever designed. I think if he was here today, he would fall in love with it as I have.

We ended the second season in great shape. It was coming out better than I expected. When standing inside the house, one could look through the windows and not see any part of the house, only the lake.

CHAPTER XXXI

Completing The Massaro House The Wright Way

Over the winter, while I was in Florida, I put together the finish schedule. A complete list of all the items we needed to finish as well as the products we needed to complete these items. When it was completed, we purchased everything we needed so we would be ready in the spring.

By mid-March, we were back on the island, ready to go to work. The roofers started working on the roofing. We ordered a special color rubber roof; it was green in color to match what the copper would eventually look like when it turned green. I wanted to start installing the handrails up the entrance stairway. I called my friend Gino, who was the president of the Sheet Metal Workers Local Union, and asked him if he wanted to help. While we were working on the handrail, he saw the roofers working on the roof. He asked if they were Union workers. I said,

"Of course they are." A few minutes later, he asked me what Union they were from. I stopped working, looked at him, and told him,

"The Soviet Union, and you'll be happy to know that all the ductwork was installed by your Union."

"Who?"

"I did it all," I said. Gino just shook his head and kept working.

In the construction industry, the last 10% of the job took an additional 20% of the time. Everything on the job was a little different than in a normal house construction job. For instance, the hand railings Gino and I were working on were to be triangular-shaped with lighting built into them. To get what I wanted and for them to feel good, we made about six different samples. The original house design did not have air conditioning. When I designed the system, I designed it so you would not know where the air conditioning was coming from; you could feel it. All the ductwork and air handlers were hidden in the outside soffits. It was like Frank Lloyd Wright designed the soffits just for that purpose. On the air outlet grills, I had them use the African Mahogany wood and cut slots in it for the air to come out so you wouldn't notice them. We needed chimney caps to stop the snow and water from coming into the house. Each chimney on the roof was a different shape. I found a company in Chicago to build them in copper as per each shape of the chimney.

The original plan called for Lydia to build all the furniture and cabinetry on site. I changed my mind at the end of last season for two reasons. One, we could save a lot of time by building them in Freddy's shop over the winter. Second, Freddy did such a nice job on the doors and windows; I didn't think we could get that quality in the field. By the time spring came, Freddy had most of the items built. We started moving the furniture on pontoon boats to the island. All of the built-in furniture was shown on the original drawings. They included all the bedrooms built-ins, kitchen cabinets, the long benches in the living room and dining room, the countertops in the bathrooms, a dining room table and chairs, and miscellaneous tables throughout the house. We used Lydia's crew to do the installation on the job site. We decided to use concrete for the countertops in the kitchen; we poured them in place.

My wife Barbara picked out all the fabrics for the benches and chairs using colors and patterns we found in several of Frank Lloyd Wright's books. She also designed four large octagon rugs with geometric patterns that we ordered from India to place throughout the living area. For several months I was talking to the town about putting a helicopter landing pad on the roof. I could not get a decision from them one way or the other. I hired a consultant who told me, "If there were no regulations in the town for a helipad, then the FAA would be in charge." We submitted the required paperwork to the FAA, and within weeks we received the approval. I called Gino to come and help me lay it out on the roof. We laid out the helipad on the roof as per their instructions with white paint. It was a 20-foot diameter circle with the smaller circle in the middle, an arrow giving you the northerly direction, and the name of the heliport 96ny. The FAA sent an inspector to the island to check it out. He approved it on the spot. We had landed about six helicopters to date, and every pilot loved the approach.

We were finally getting close to completing the magnificent house. I started to make plans for the big party we wanted to throw to introduce our family and friends to the island. It was going to include all of our family, lifelong friends, and everybody that helped us bring this project to life. We were even inviting the original owner Mrs. Chahroudi and her son Dod. The party was a great success. Everybody loved the house. I was ready for everyone to get off my island so I could relax for a few days and soak in all that we had just completed.

Every day I saw something different in the house; it could be an angle on the wall or a view from the living room, or how the light came into the room. The other thing that made it a very special place was the island itself. It was an 11-acre heart-shaped island. Just a couple of years ago, I realized that it is an old-growth forest on the island. Most of the trees are Beechnut because of the rocky island itself. The roots do not go down; they go out. I found a formula on the Internet that calculated how old the trees are without cutting them. It turns out we have trees older than the country itself. My oldest tree goes back to 1769. There's a trail all the way around the island and thousands of different views of the lake from that trail.

Since I completed the house, we have done dozens of fundraisers out there for different groups. We have shown the house to at least 1000 people. One thing in common with all the visitors is that when they walk through the front door and see the skylight area with a huge rock in there, you can hear them all take a deep breath. People ask me all the time how much it cost to build the house. I give everybody the same answer. Frank Lloyd Wright's budget was at 50,000 dollars. I went over his budget. It was one hell of a project. Just like all the rest of the big jobs I took in my business, when I look back at this job, it too was over my head, but I got it completed. It actually came out better than I expected. The foundation will not recognize the house because I would not pay the 450,000 dollars that they tried to extort from me. I don't understand how the president of the Frank Lloyd Wright Foundation won't even come out to look at the house. He doesn't have to like it; as a matter of fact, he could tear it apart, but I think as the president, he's obligated to come and look at this house.

According to Frank's own words, "When the house on the island is completed, it will be more beautiful than my Fallingwater." Some of the Frank Lloyd Wright purists believe the house should not have been built because Frank was not alive; therefore, it can't be a Frank Lloyd Wright house. Frank only visited 1/3 of the homes he designed. Does that mean the other 2/3 are not Frank Lloyd Wright houses? Of course, they are, and so is this one. This house is built closer to Frank Lloyd Wright's original drawings than any other house he ever built. The reason is; on the other houses he built, the owners requested changes after the drawings were completed… like a bigger kitchen or an additional closet. I made no changes to the original drawings. No matter what the foundation says, they can't change the fact that this house is Frank Lloyd Wright's masterpiece, and I built it. It is absolutely breathtaking. Frank was a genius, and I'm really happy I got to complete his masterpiece.

CHAPTER XXXII

New Idea For An Old Company

Mike, from the restaurant in Lake Placid, was having trouble making the mortgage payments. With Obama in the White House, it didn't look like there would ever be a recovery. We were under threat of losing the building to the bank, and I couldn't let that happen, so I took over the loan myself. Years went by with no financial improvement, so we decided it was time to sell the building. No buildings had been selling at that time, especially restaurants. We had not had an offer for several years. We were approached by Subway to rent part of the building to them, and we agreed. Subway finally moved in, and we started getting some rent. Not nearly enough to pay the overhead, though. I put myself in that mess for almost 15 years. I wasn't going to whine about it. Instead, I picked myself up, dug in my heels, and found a way to limit my losses. After all, it wasn't my first rodeo in Lake Placid!

***

In 2017, my good friend Brad McDowe (Eggplant) passed away. Eggplant and I had a connection that most people didn't understand. We helped each other. I miss him very much. After the wake, I stopped to visit my lawyer Charlie Walsh. Charlie said to me, "Hey, Joe. There is a guy buying up everything in Lake Placid and Saranac Lake. He bought the AP shopping center, the old post office, and bought a building in Lake Placid. I heard that the building he has in Lake Placid doesn't have enough parking. Maybe you should approach him and see if he wants to rent some of the restaurant parking lot, and that might lead to a sale."

He gave me his telephone number. His name was Palo, and he owned a small pizza place in Saranac Lake. I called Palo immediately. I did not take Charlie's advice to talk to Palo about a parking lot. Instead, I went directly for the sale, typical Joe! I said,

"Palo, you don't know me. I'm a friend of Mike Nichols. We own the restaurant "Nicole's on Main Street." Do you know that building?"

"Yes, I do!"

"I am looking to sell it, maybe you would be interested."

"Joe, I have so many projects going on right now that I could not think about another. Give me your telephone number and you never know down the road what might happen."

I gave him my number. About two weeks went by until I called Palo. I said,

"Palo, every once in a while a deal comes across your desk and no matter how busy you are, it's a deal you can't turn down." Before he could say anything, I told him I would sell him our building for under 2 million dollars. We both knew that the building was worth more than double that number. After a long pause, he asked me,

"How much under 2 million dollars?"

I said to him, "Let's meet and walk through the restaurant to see if it fits your needs, then we'll talk."

A couple of weeks later, we met at the restaurant. I met with Palo and his son, but his partner from Canada could not make it. He must've been the money guy. Palo told me they wanted the building for an Airbnb and a smaller restaurant. As we were walking through, he said to me that all the fancy walls and ceilings would have to come out. He mentioned it would be a lot of work for him, and he kept going on and on and on. I knew that he was pointing that out because he wanted to negotiate the price. Finally, I said to him,

"Palo, if the building doesn't fit your needs, I don't care how good a deal is, you can't buy it."

When we were finished, Palo invited me to his other restaurant. Palo thought he was a good negotiator, but what he didn't know was that he was in my wheelhouse now. I went in to talk to Mike before going to Palo's restaurant. I said to Mike, "The dance starts now." I met Palo at his restaurant; we sat down to have a cup of coffee. He said,

"Joe, I want to make an offer on the building."

"Palo, your partner is not here, I don't want to negotiate twice." He assured me that he was the one who made financial decisions. I said, "Okay, I will sell you the building for 1,800,000 dollars."

Palo said, "I don't want to insult you with what I want to pay you for this building."

"You can't insult me, what's the number?"

"1,500,000 dollars."

I said, "Palo, before I gave you the number of $1,800,000 I said to myself, *Palo is a sophisticated buyer, just go to your best number. He knows what a bargain it is, and that's what we will sell the building for.* I could've started at 1,950,000 dollars, but instead I didn't want to screw around and went right to the number that I can accept."

"I can't go above 1.5 million dollars and you can't go below $1.8 million."

"So, Palo," I said. "You have my number. Tomorrow I'll put it on the market for 1,800,000 dollars and will see what happens." I sat back and waited about five minutes. Then I said to him, "Or we can split the difference of 1,650,000 dollars and put this to bed."

He went to say something, but I stopped him and said, "Palo, you know what kind of deal this is, either now or never." He looked at me, and we shook hands on the deal. I was never so happy in my life to lose money. This albatross was not around my neck anymore, or was it?

The contracts were completed, and we set a closing date. All I had to do was sign the contract and mail it back from Florida by the closing date. The closing was set for Friday in Lake Placid. I didn't receive the paperwork until the Wednesday before. They were held up because of a snowstorm, so I notarized and signed the papers and then went to Federal Express. They told me they could definitely get the papers there by Friday morning for the closing. On Friday morning, I got a call that the paperwork was not there. I checked with Federal Express, and they told me the paperwork was stuck someplace in the Midwest because of the same storm. I called my lawyer back and told them what happened, and they rescheduled the closing for the following Monday. I didn't want to take any chances, so I had my lawyer send me another set of documents just in case the other never showed up.

Lake Placid was not through with me, though. On Saturday morning, I got a call from Mike. He told me that they had four feet of snow the day before, and yesterday they had a meltdown. The roof drains were frozen. The water poured in and ruined the kitchen ceilings, some ceilings in the restaurant, and some other damages. I called Palo and told him what happened. He told me he had other buildings in town doing the same thing and not to worry about it until we close on Monday. "We will just put a contingency in for the cost of the repairs," he said. Late Saturday afternoon, I got a call from Mike. He said that the temperatures were going down to the under -20 range, and three of the four heaters were not working. He couldn't get anybody to fix the heating system. We were afraid the sprinkler system would freeze. He ran all around town to pick up portable heaters to try to keep the place from freezing solid.

I never received the new sale contracts for the restaurant from Federal Express. It all had to do with the winter storm that was affecting everything. The contracts finally showed up late Saturday. I went to Federal Express and asked them what was the latest time I could send them out to get there on Monday morning by 10. They told me if I had it there by 1 pm on Sunday, it would still make the closing. I went to Federal Express on Sunday morning to get the papers notarized. Federal Express did not notarize. It was Sunday morning, and every place that notarizes was closed. Someone told me that the UPS store had a notary on standby. I ran up to the UPS store and got the contract notarized, then ran back to Federal Express in time to get them out for the closing on Monday morning. We kept the building from freezing that night and got the heating system up the next day. Closing was finally done, and I was done with Lake Placid. I promise I don't care how good of a deal comes along... I learned my lesson, I hope!

***

East Coast had been in business for almost 30 years. For most
of the 30 years, it had been the leader in its industry. The one thing
that slowed us down was the patent infringement case that we lost.
We had been operating under that patent for years. Now that patent
was coming to an end and it could mean great things for East Coast
Sheet Metal. There were a lot of other companies coming into our
marketplace. Technology had been moving a lot faster now, and it
became hard to keep up with it. AutoCAD was the big player in the
market now. Most large architectural and engineering firms were
using AutoCAD. My CAD software was operating under a
different operating system than AutoCAD. Our competition had
been writing their products using AutoCAD. The large construction
manager companies and the engineer companies were writing in
their specification that all CAD software must be AutoCAD
compatible. Even though our software was leaps and bounds ahead
of the competition, it was not being written under AutoCAD, so we
were not keeping up with the competition. We had a conversion
program that allowed us to be integrated with the AutoCAD
software, but it was not the same as being in AutoCAD. It was not
only hurting our CAD sales but also our duct fabrication and
piping programs. For us to be a force in the industry, we were
going to have to make some big changes.

We were showing our CAD package at the annual HVAC
show. It just happened that the booth next to ours was AutoCAD's

booth, showing their latest CAD product. It was called M.E.P.
(Mechanical, Electrical, Plumbing), and the program would
become the industry-standard. I told my salesman and my son-in-
law that I was going to go over to make a deal with AutoCAD; of
course, they laughed at me. It was the first day of the show, and the
crowd had not reached our booth yet. I went over to the AutoCAD
booth and asked for a demo. The demonstrator went through it and
gave me a complete demo of their duct CAD system. When he
finished, I asked him if he could fabricate. He said, "No we can't,
and everybody keeps asking us about that." So I invited him over
for a demo of our system. When we finished the demo, he asked if
he could bring his boss over the next day for a demo. I said, "Sure
let's do that."

The next day, he came over to our booth with his boss, and I
gave them a complete demo of our system. At the end of the demo,
the boss said, "We would be very interested in working with you
guys." It just so happened that their main headquarters was in
Boston, not far from where Dave's shop was. I sat down with Dave
and our programming team to kick around a few ideas of how we
could interact with the MEP AutoCAD drawing. We came up with
an idea and asked our program department to make us a small
demo program. The demo program would show a couple of pieces
of straight ductwork connecting to a radius elbow. If we could
accomplish it, it would prove that we could include fabrication

instructions inside their program. We set up a meeting with AutoCAD to show them our demo. There were three people from AutoCAD in that meeting. One of them was the fellow whom I gave the demo to at the show. After the meeting, he said it looked really good and wondered if we could expand on it further. We said we could do that.

Over the next couple of weeks, we expanded the program to be able to give a larger demo. We brought our demo back to AutoCAD when it was complete. At the meeting, there were eight people from AutoCAD. At the end of the demo, the boss asked each person on his team if their product could do what they just saw. Every one of them said they could not. He said they wanted to work with us to complete the program. They also told us that they could not give us an exclusive contract. Dave and I were concerned about that, but I told Dave, "Let's do the job anyway, we have nothing to lose." We needed to be tied in with AutoCAD. We set up a software team that would work right inside Autodesk programs; it could take several months. We were ready with our program in time for the big HVAC show coming up.

The program allowed us to have an AutoCAD based sheet metal and piping drawing system. The only problem with the system that I saw was that we still had to redraw the ductwork from the mechanical drawings. It seemed like such a waste of time that the engineer already drew the ductwork, and we had to draw it again. When an engineer draws ductwork, he's drawing what we call "dumb ductwork." It knows nothing about the fabrication requirements. After, we had to add that information when we redrew it into our system. They represented the ductwork correctly when drawing in a 3-D model; *why can't we just use the ductwork they already drew?*

While watching my guys give the demo of our new product at the HVAC show, I started asking our programmer some questions; remember Ilia? The young Russian kid I met way back at the beginning? Well, he was my programmer there, so my first question was:

"Could we find a piece of duct in their drawing with the MEP program? As in… do we know the location of a piece of duct inside the software?"

He said, "Yes, we know the exact location of the duct within our program."

"Does our program know what the duct was?"

He said, "Yes, our program knows it's a piece of ductwork."

"Does the program know what type of duct it was? Like, if it's an elbow or a piece of pipe?"

"Yes, we know what it is."

"Then why the hell do we have to redraw every piece of their ductwork if our program knows where and what it is? Why don't we convert their dumb duct inside our program without redrawing it?"

Ilia looked at me as the lightbulb went off in his head and said, "I think we can."

If we could pull this off, it would be industry-changing. It was time for another program rewrite. I wanted Ilia and his team to write a small program proving that we could make this work. A couple of weeks later, he showed me a demo of how exactly we could do it. There was a new competitor in our marketplace. They had been working in England for years. They stayed out of America because the CAD product was patented. With the CAD patent expiring, they were setting up salespeople in America. Their program was already written in Autodesk. There were several rumors that Autodesk was interested in buying them.

I talked with David and told him that everybody would copy it if we wrote the new product. We needed to see if we could get a patent on it. I had been screwed by patent infringement once before; now it was our turn to use patent law in our favor! Dave and I met with patent lawyers in New York City. There were two patents already out there on CAD. The Lavine patent, which covered fabrication, and the other patent covered 3-D modeling. We had to convince these lawyers that our patent was completely different than the other two. After several meetings with our lawyers, they believed that the system we were proposing could be patentable. We went to work on two fronts: getting the program up and running, and the other, writing up the patent.

In October 2005, we filed for a US patent. We called the program Design-to-Fabrication. We could take any engineering drawing that was drawn in AutoCAD MEP and electronically transfer it to estimating without doing a physical takeoff and fabricate without redrawing. It was industry changing. We could spend weeks estimating a job which would limit how many jobs we could estimate because of the time restraints. Instead of spending weeks getting an estimate out, we could do it in days with that system. Producing the fabricated drawings for piping and ductwork would take no time; instead of spending months completing these drawings, we would spend days.

It took over a year before we heard from the US Patent Department. The news was not good; they turned our patent down. We sat with our lawyers and went over every detail. They believed that with a few changes in the patent, we could get approval. The next thing we knew, the patent examiner (who was working on our program) had left, and we were assigned a new examiner. We made the changes and resubmitted the patent for approval. Another year went by before we heard from the patent department. They rejected our patent for the second time! The lawyers told me we could make a couple of small changes and try one more time. They told me if it was rejected a third time, then we were done; they were out of ideas. We spent hundreds of thousands of dollars trying to get the patent approved. Without the patent, the competitors would copy the program instantly. Another year went by before we got the bad news from the patent department that our changes had still been rejected. We met with the lawyers, and they said they had no more ideas on how to make our product patentable. We were done.

Time for plan Z. I asked the lawyers if we could meet with the new examiner. They said it was possible, probably not helpful. I said, "Let's go for it." A couple of weeks later, Dave, myself, and our lawyer met in Washington DC. As I was walking through the security check at the patent office, I saw a man on the other side of security looking at me. When I got through, he said to me,

"Are you the inventor?"

I said, "Yes, I am."

"I love inventors, my father was an inventor."

I smiled and thought to myself; I *can negotiate with this guy.* We headed up to his office, where we shared copies of the other two patents and some drawings that we produced. I put my drawing on the bench and the other patent on each side of my drawing. Then, I began to explain to the examiner that the first patent produced a 3-D drawing, and the other patent produced a fabrication file. My patent was in between both of those other patents. He looked at everything and said, "Oh! I see what you mean. Stand over there and I'll tell your lawyer how to write it up, so it passes."

In March of 2011, our patent was finally approved. East Coast CAD/CAM entered a new world. We owned the patent on industry changing technology. At the big shows, we were inside the Autodesk booth working with them. Just like I predicted, the English company copied our program and started marketing it. We put them on notice that they were infringing on our patent. Their representative called me and wanted to explain to me why they were not infringing on my patent. He kept talking and talking about why they were not infringing, and I kept telling him they were indeed infringing. Finally, I said to him, "Let me be perfectly clear, even if you're not infringing you're infringing," and I ended the conversation.

Their argument was that the main company was in England. The company selling the product here in the United States was nothing but a sales outlet. I could not sue the company in England because my patent was for the U.S. If I sued the sales company and won, they would close up and have no money, and I would end up with nothing. I had to give this some thought and figure out how we could stop them. Things were going along pretty well. Our products were getting great reviews. I was in Florida when I got a call from David. He said,

"Sit down Joe, you are not going to believe this. I was just called into a meeting with Autodesk. They told me that they will not be working with us any longer because they bought the company from England."

I could not believe this, but I was not surprised about it though. It was what big companies did. That was why we got the patent in the first place. We were headed into another bumpy road; I should've been used to it by now!

CHAPTER XXXIII

When Someone Gives Lemons, You Make Lemonade

After our initial shock from the Autodesk news, I started kicking some things around. The next day, I called David, who was sick over the surprise, and I told him they just gave us the biggest gift. You see, we couldn't sue CADduct, the English company, for infringement because they weren't infringing on our US patent, but Autodesk just bought them, so now Autodesk was infringing. The problem was that we were a small company, and Autodesk was huge. There was no way we would financially survive a long-drawn-out court case. I needed to find a lawyer who would take the case on contingency. AutoDesk was planning on us backing down because they believed we could not afford to fight. I didn't typically back down.

I started doing some searching on the Internet for a contingency lawyer. I talked to a couple of the firms, but none of them seemed interested. I happened to be talking to my architect Tom Heinz one day and told him about the situation with Autodesk. He told me that he had done some work in a building in Chicago for a contingency lawyer who handled patent infringement cases. Who's the luckiest guy? I gave him a call to introduce myself and told him a little bit about our predicament. He told me he was coming up to the Northeast in about a week, and he would be willing to meet at our Boston office.

***

Meet Rolf Stadheim, the owner of the law firm Stadheim and Griear. He met us at our office with his partner Joe. We gave them a demo of our product and showed them the Lavine patent. Their specialty was contingency patent infringement for universities, but they would also take unusual cases like this one. What he liked about our case was that Lavine was getting a royalty of 10,000 dollars per workstation for his patent. The other thing he liked was that the industry was used to paying a royalty. He said they would give it some thought and get back to us.

I received a call from my friend Joe Nigro; he was my counterpart on the National Labor Relations Board. He was now president of the Sheet Metal Workers International Union. He told me that the craft training fund, which the Union supported, was working on a program similar to mine and that he would like me to stop by and take a look at it since he spent hundreds of thousands of dollars on it. I told him I would set up a meeting with them. Dave and I went to a meeting at the Union in Washington DC. We went into a conference room expecting to see a computer and a demo. Two guys were in there and started talking to us about our program. I realized they were not going to show us the program, and Joe Nigro was out of town. They knew about my patent, and somehow the conversation came around about them buying us. I thought it was just a ploy to get us out of the meeting, but the guy said, "Go back and come up with the number."

I said, "Let me have your business card."

He gave it to me. I wrote the number on the back of his business cards and slid the card over to him. The number was 20 million dollars. He looked at it and said he would talk to Joe about it. I didn't think much of it, then we left. I was at the airport when Joe Nigro called me and asked me how the meeting went. I told him they wouldn't show me the program. He was not a happy camper and dropped more F-bombs than I had heard in a long time. Then I told him about their offer for purchase.

He said, "When I get back to Washington, I'll give you a call."

A couple of days later, Joe called me, and we started talking about their CAD product. Joe told me they started the project before he was president. Their idea was to offer the program for free if they would join the Union. Joe started telling me they were spending hundreds of thousands of dollars on this project. I told him there were two problems with this: number one, the price of CAD had dropped tremendously, and number two, my new design to fabrication program would eventually make the other CAD obsolete. I said to him,

"If you buy my company, you will own the patent. The only way anybody would be able to use the technology would be through you."

Joe said to me, "Let me look into it with my people. You may have to come down and give us a demo of it."

I said, "Joe, that's no problem. Anytime you just call me, and we'll be there."

A week later, we went to Washington for a meeting with the Union. It was Dave, myself, and our patent lawyer. They had their house lawyer and a couple of guys I met the last time I was there. We gave them a full blown demonstration of design and fabrication. It was really impressive. The next hour, the two lawyers went back and forth on how strong the patent was. At the end of the meeting, I was called into Joe's office, and he said to me,

"I need a little time to convince our board. This could take me a few weeks."

I said, "No problem, Joe. Whatever you need, let me know."

Around the same time, the contingency lawyer called me and said they would be interested in taking the case against AutoCAD, but we had to pay the expenses. I told Rolf Stadheim that I was in possible negotiations with the Union about selling my company and that I would have to wait and see how that came out before I would go forward with the lawsuit. He said he understood and to let him know if and when we were ready. I thanked him and said I would get back to him. If only I knew then what I know now. Timing is everything

Joe Nigro called me and said he had bad news. He had convinced his board members to buy us, but their Union just merged with the railroad Union, and their board members turned it down. He said he really wanted it. He did not want to be known as the president that lost drafting in the industry! It would've been a great deal for us, but you can't win them all. Time to go to plan Z again. I gave a call to Roff and said, "Let's go, let's go kick AutoCAD's butt."

We got ourselves some contingency lawyers. Rolf called Autodesk to set up a meeting with their lawyers in California before we filed the lawsuit. We flew out to meet at their main headquarters in California. They were right when they said they had two whole floors of lawyers. Rolf's pitch was that the industry was used to paying royalties on this type of technology, pointing out how well Levin did with his patent. We offered them exclusive rights to our patent. After our meeting, they said they would get back to us. It didn't take long before they said they were not interested and would see us in court. When you take a lawsuit like this on, especially with a company that makes 3 billion dollars a year, it takes on a life of its own. They say there's only one way to get a patent but thousands of ways to defeat a patent.

Dave and I flew to Chicago for our first meeting with our law firm. Their office was in the penthouse of the famous Wrigley Building. Joe, Rolf's partner, ran the day-to-day operations of the law firm. Rolf was pretty much retired. We started talking about the case and came up with a strategy. We were going to need expert witnesses and financial guys to figure out the damages. Whatever Autodesk had sold since the patent was issued would be considered damages. If it was willful infringement, which it was, it could be multiplied times three. We guesstimated what the damages could possibly be; the number we came up with was in excess of 40 million dollars. *It could be my biggest deal ever,* I thought. It would be a long road between the meeting and the final outcome. We decided to sue them in Rhode Island Supreme Court. I was told that we could be in that court faster than any other, approximately one year. At the end of the meeting, we felt pretty good about the team and our approach to the lawsuit.

CHAPTER XXXIV

Sometimes You Just Get Lemons

The case seemed to be moving along. We hired an expert witness. He was a college professor who taught financing. Rolf called to tell me his partner Joe had suddenly passed away. He said he had to come out of retirement and take over running the law firm. The first thing he did was change the lawyers that had been working with Joe on our case, which pushed the lawsuit back until everybody caught up to speed. David and I flew back out to Chicago to meet the new group.

Meet George Summerfield, the new lawyer on our case. My first impressions of George were not the greatest. It seemed that we had to convince him our patent was valid. It took several weeks to get back on track. In the meantime, Autodesk lawyers kept bringing motions to the court to get the case thrown out. So far, they hadn't been able to do that; our case was holding up. Lately, the courts had been inundated by patent lawsuits on computer programming. What had been happening was, some people had been writing short algorithm routines and patenting them. When a company tried to use the algorithm, they were sued for patent infringement; it was clogging up the court system.

There had been one case like that which moved all the way up to the Supreme Court. The name of that case was Alice. It had to do with mathematical algorithms and routine software patents. We were about two weeks away from our trial in Rhode Island, so I went out to buy some winter clothes since I lived in Florida most winters by then. There was one more hearing coming before the court case where Autodesk brought up the Alice patent as a defense against the loss. After the hearing, David called me to say he thought it went pretty well and that we would know shortly. A week later, I was playing poker when I received a call from David. He said, "Joe, we just got the decision. The courts just threw our case out."

He was not kidding. The Supreme Court decided that computer program patents, in general, were no longer valid. The courts said that just because you can use a computer to do something that you could previously only do by hand, did not make it patentable. The Supreme Court had thrown out thousands of patents that were real. It was a major setback for East Coast CADCAM. Without the protection of the patent, we couldn't compete any longer in the market. Between paying the expenses on the lawsuit and the money we had invested into the new programs, I had spent approximately 2 million dollars. We still had the best program out there, but we couldn't compete with big corporations without the protection of our patent. What these big companies were doing was dropping the price to drive the little guys out of business. It would be too big of a gamble to invest more money. The company and the products that we developed helped me grow our sheet metal company into one of the largest companies in my area. David had done a magnificent job running the company, and I really enjoyed working with him. But losing the case was really the end of East Coast.

We needed to come up with a plan to give David a future outside of East Coast. We had been working with a company named Trimble for several years. We had incorporated some of their products into our programming. We tied their laser pointer into our CAD product. On the job site, that feature allowed us to shoot a laser pointer where we would need to put a hanger for ductwork or piping. It so happened that Autodesk was their biggest competitor. A few years earlier, they were interested in selling our products. At the time, we were not interested because of our patent. We then approached them to license them the use of our patent. They wanted to wait to see how the lawsuit turned out, which was very smart of them. After hearing about the failed lawsuit, they contacted us and wanted us to come out to Denver to talk with them. Both David and I were pretty deflated after our huge patent loss, but we couldn't mope around forever; we had to get back up, brush off, and see what was next. It was not my first failure, but it was David's.

He and I flew out to Denver to meet with Trumble. What they wanted was to take over our sales, marketing, customer support, documentation, and subscriptions. They would leave us to continue programming and maintaining our product. They offered us a 50-50 split on new sales and 60% over subscription revenue. They wanted our product to compete against Autodesk. We needed the financial assistance and the sales support. We loved the idea that our product would still be competing against Autodesk. We told them that we would go back and give it some thought. We knew we had to do it, but we didn't want to jump on it. On the flight back, we decided to take the deal, and it worked that way for two years.

After the second year, Trumble decided they wanted to buy the product from us and take David to work with them. It wasn't the 20 million dollar number that we were once so close to, but it was enough to pay down some of the debt, give a nice chunk to David, and get David a secure job. David was now in charge of all their CAD products. He continued to work from Boston and had more vacation time than when we worked together. In the end, it was a good deal.

As for me…retirement isn't all that's cracked up to be. I am just waiting for the next crazy idea to appear!

CHAPTER XXXV

The Reason For My Success Is Stupidity

Most of the time, when I did something that people thought was stupid, what I would hear was, "What's wrong with you?" I tried to come up with a logical reason why I have always been that way. The honest answer is… I have no idea. I honestly didn't think there was anything wrong with me. I was talking with one of my competitors about business one day; he was a college graduate who majored in Business Administration. During our conversation, he told me that once his company would cover their overhead expense, they would drop their bid price by the amount of the overhead. He learned that tactic in college. I looked at it differently. Once I covered my overhead and reached my profit objective, I would raise my bid price. I figured that if I had more work than I could handle, I was willing to give up a job if I wasn't going to make a lot of money on it. I'm so glad I missed that class. When we were lucky enough to win a big job, we would have to sign a legal document with many restrictions. Sometimes, my competitor would refuse to sign the document. I would take the job and worry about it later. I liked to cross bridges when I got to them.

It's obvious my mind works differently than the minds of other people. It's obvious that I'm not stupid, but there are just certain things I can't learn. Spelling is one of them. If you remember, when I was a little boy, I wrote down all my spelling words, cut them into little pieces, and stuck them onto the bottom of the coffee table. Now we all realize it would've been easier for me to learn to spell the words. I guess that part of my brain is malfunctioning. Some very famous people, I am sure you have heard of, were really bad spellers: George Washington, Winston Churchill, Andrew Jackson, John F. Kennedy, Ernest Hemingway, Albert Einstein, F. Scott Fitzgerald, Agatha Christie, and Jane Austin.

I think my brain compensates for the things I have a difficult time learning, which gets me through life, like the ability to see things that are not obvious to other people or the ability to make quick decisions without fear of failure. Remember when I was working in the shop on the dumb end of the power brakes with a man who'd been doing it for 20 years? I saw a way to eliminate one die change after working for just an hour. Once, while at the airport, I noticed a food delivery truck lifting an entire box to service an airplane. I went to an airport and found out how I could buy a used one to deliver my ductwork to the buildings' second floor. While I was at an HVAC show, I noticed a man operating a machine that was cutting different patterns in sheet-metal.

I said to my uncle Vince, "Look at that machine. We could use that to cut radius elbows." He said I was right, and we purchased the machine off the floor. We eventually started building these machines and selling them to other sheet metal shops. While installing our coil line for fabricating straight ducts sections, I said to the technician from the Lock Former Company, "We could use this machine to make transitions." He said to me, "This machine only makes straight sections of ductwork." I showed him how we could put an extra notch in the straight section of the duct and take it to the shear to become a transition. He was as surprised as everybody else.

We won a large cleanroom job at IBM, which required every piece of ductwork to be cleaned, fabricated, with the ends covered in plastic. It was the largest and most expensive part of the job, resulting in fabrication costs being 30-40% higher than normal, and delivery costs that were three times more. What I ended up doing was cut all the ductwork, cleaned it, leaving it in the flat position without bending, putting them on pallets, plastic wrap the pallets, and finally shipping the pallets. Then I bought all the new equipment that I needed to fabricate the ductwork, cleaned it, and installed it in the cleanroom, where I did all the final fabrication. People often say, "Sometimes you need to think outside of the box." I never saw the box. I just saw the easiest way to accomplish things.

It took me ten years, from the time I bought Elmsford Sheet Metal from my uncle to building one of the best and most profitable HVAC companies in the United States, that employed over 350 Union workers. It took Pennsylvania Power & Light company two years to tank my company down to only 50 employees and only 18 years to put Elmsford Sheet Metal out of business. With all their high-powered executives with fancy titles and degrees, they said, "I was not corporate material." Thank God for that.

After I sold my company, I tried to keep myself busy. I bought a new building for East Coast Sheet Metal. I partnered with my friend Mike up in Lake Placid to build a new building with two restaurants. I partnered with my friend Frank Candela and bought four condos in Fort Myers, Florida, when the market was hot. I bought a new SL 500 Mercedes, which I traded a year later for a 2003 BMW Z8 that I still have today. I bought a 20-foot twin-engine speed boat for Florida. We renovated the townhouse in Florida. After I moved East Coast Sheet Metal to Boston so my son-in-law could run it, I came up with the idea of a new design-to-fabrication program and spent quite a bit of time getting it patented and fighting lawsuits.

Over the last couple of years, I started liquidating many of my assets. I sold my half ownership in the two buildings in Peekskill back to my uncle, who wanted it for his three daughters. I sold the original building that housed East Coast Sheet Metal. I also sold the four condos in Florida and the building in Fishkill. Then, I sold a restaurant in Lake Placid and finally sold East Coast Sheet Metal.

The largest asset I still own is Petra Island with the Frank Lloyd Wright masterpiece. I spend most of my summers out there, and the more time I spend there, the more I see how fantastic the house and the island are. I just turned 74. It's a good time to sit back and enjoy the fruits of my labor, or maybe I have one more great idea in me —just one more crazy idea.

In 1945, Frank Lloyd Wright designed a health spa for Elizabeth Arden to be built at the base of the Camelback Mountains in Arizona. The project was never built...yet! One thing is for sure; it's been a hell of a ride, and I think the bottom line is asking yourself, "If you were allowed to do it all over again, without making any changes, would you do it?" For me...

Absolutely yes!

ABOUT THE AUTHOR

 Joe Massaro was born into a working class Italian family from New York. Growing up, he struggled with school but later learned of his talents in the sheet metal industry after working for his uncle Vincent. He saw his career take off from apprentice to owner of the Elmsford Sheet Metal Works, the largest privately owned sheet metal company in the six counties north of New York City. He now spends his time in Mahopac, NY, at the Frank Lloyd Wright home on Petra Island and his beachfront property in Florida.

First seat on the left

My mom and me

My youngest daughter Jennifer with my wife
and my oldest daughter Donna

My family

Natural rock outcropping of George Washing face on Petra Island

Joe with Walter Cronkite on Petra Island

Actor John Amos and I at an award ceremony for him.
A frequent visitor to Petra Island

Joe Bo and I at the barber shop in Lake
Placid during the Olympics

Helicopter on roof of Frank Lloyd Wright house

Lonnie and I at a computer show

My architect, my builder, and me

Opening party for the house

My builder Lydia, myself, and Tom the architect

Building inspector, my architect, and me

My wife and me

Original owner's son and wife

Building inspector and my architect

Lightning Source UK Ltd.
Milton Keynes UK
UKHW022354120821
388717UK00010B/504/J